Internal Affairs

Internal Affairs

A JOURNALKEEPING WORKBOOK FOR SELF-INTIMACY

Kay Leigh Hagan
Feb. 17, 1990

*For Mary Louise,
thanks for sharing
a special evening
with me... now
Start!*

PERENNIAL LIBRARY

HARPER & ROW, PUBLISHERS, SAN FRANCISCO

NEW YORK, GRAND RAPIDS, PHILADELPHIA, ST. LOUIS
LONDON, SINGAPORE, SYDNEY, TOKYO, TORONTO

Kay Leigh Hagan offers workshops and lectures nationally. For a schedule of upcoming appearances, or for information on sponsoring one in your area, please write c/o Escapadia Press, 454 Seminole Ave., NE, #6, Atlanta, GA, 30307.

INTERNAL AFFAIRS: *A Journalkeeping Workbook for Self-Intimacy.* Copyright © 1990, 1988 by Kay Leigh Hagan. All rights reserved. Printed in the United States of America. No part of this book may be used or reproduced in any manner whatsoever without written permission except in the case of brief quotations embodied in critical articles and reviews. For information address Harper & Row, Publishers, Inc., 10 East 53rd Street, New York, NY 10022.

FIRST HARPER & ROW EDITION PUBLISHED IN 1990.

Illustration by Linda Finnell
Design by Paula Schlosser

LIBRARY OF CONGRESS CATALOGING-IN-PUBLICATION DATA
Hagan, Kay Leigh.
    Internal affairs : a journalkeeping workbook for self-intimacy /
Kay Leigh Hagan.—1st Harper & Row ed.
        p. cm.
    Includes bibliographical references.
    ISBN 0-06-250371-5
    1. Self-perception—Problems, exercises, etc. 2. Diaries-
-Authorship.   I. Title.
BF697.5.S43H34   1990
158′. 1—dc20   89-45753
                                                               CIP

90 91 92 93 94 RRD 10 9 8 7 6 5 4 3 2 1

CONTENTS

INTRODUCTION

WHEN I BEGAN CONDUCTING journalkeeping workshops in 1981, I felt that journalkeeping—a personal habit of twenty years—was the single most influential and stable quality of my life. To it I attributed my ability to hear the voice of my heart. At that time, the how and why of this power was still a mystery to me but as I searched for ways to motivate others to keep journals, the mysterious power of writing for self-reflection became obvious. Listening to my inner voice, becoming familiar with my deepest concerns, grounds me first in myself. All other decisions are then based in a firm knowledge and awareness of my own being. While this may seem unnecessarily basic to some, I am convinced by eight years of workshops and several hundred participants that conscious, consistent self-intimacy is nothing short of revolutionary. Self-intimacy is the first step to self-empowerment.

Like the intimacies we have with others, intimacy with self evolves over time. But the growth is not linear—there is no formula or list of steps leading to the perfect relationship with self. Instead, self-intimacy emerges from shared experience. Because of this, *Internal Affairs* is a workbook with exercises that take the many aspects of sharing we do with other people and explore how to share intimately with the self. In doing so, we can create an internal relationship of acceptance, trust, nurture, healing, and magic. A journal provides a unique space for this sharing, a safe place for the mind and heart to communicate freely with each other.

A journal is tangible evidence of your relationship with self. Journalkeeping is an act of risk, disclosure, vulnerability and courage. It is also an act of self-affirmation. It is a gesture of valuing the self, of saying "I am," of demonstrating self-love by paying attention to your thoughts, actions, and feelings. On another level, journalkeeping is the mind's celebration of the heart. Using the rational system of symbols we call language, the mind records without judgement the passionate energy of the heart emerging unrestrained by fear of censure. This is an experience of absolute freedom, and intimacy.

Describing journalkeeping as a lifetime companion, *Internal Affairs* covers a broad range of journal issues, from challenging chronic excuses for not writing to discovering patterns by studying completed volumes. But this is not a "how to book" in the strictest sense, for in journalkeeping there are no rules—it's all a matter of personal choice. The goal of this workbook is to create a place for you to experiment with writing for self-reflection. *Internal Affairs* is an interim step between desire and commitment—the desire to know yourself intimately through journalkeeping, and the commitment to fill a book of blank pages with your own words. My belief is that you will like who you see reflected here, and decide to step through the mirror of the journal into a deeper intimacy—and connection—with yourself.

Kay Leigh Hagan
Atlanta, Georgia
June 19, 1989
Full Moon

AN INVITATION

THIS IS AN INVITATION for you to become not only a reader of *Internal Affairs,* but also a co-author. I encourage you to do just that by writing in this book.

To ease your way, special care has been taken in designing *Internal Affairs:* wide margins for jotting quick thoughts while reading; a heavier back cover for writing comfortably without a desk; and spiralbinding, so that pages will open perfectly flat.

Throughout the workbook, exercises offer practical experience in the different aspects of journalwriting and self-intimacy described. In addition to the exercises, I have included several questions at the end of each chapter to stimulate a personal interview— or "inner view." Asking questions is a good way to get to know someone, and I hope these questions, some of them serious, others odd and funny, will provoke thoughtful and illuminating answers. While I suspect our book will not be one that you loan to other people, I do hope you will recommend it.

My portion is completed: a basic guide to journalkeeping for self-intimacy in a workbook format. As you move through the exercises and questions, you will write your portion. In doing so, you will personalize, and complete, *Internal Affairs.*

Internal Affairs

Hope: Intimacy and Freedom

W HAT MAKES A RELATIONSHIP intimate? *Intimacy* is one of those buzzwords we use frequently without questioning its meaning. We lament the "quality of intimacy" in our lives and seem to have a clear standard of closeness, communication, and sharing that our relationships never quite reach. A common observation from people in long-term partnerships is, "We're close, but I don't feel like s/he really *knows* me." Yet I've also heard about and experienced intimacy with virtual strangers, encountered during travels for an hour or two, sharing an airline delay or something equally coincidental. What do we mean when we say intimacy?

If we turn to a standard dictionary definition, we find that intimacy refers to something that is intrinsic or essential, that characterizes one's deepest nature. Intimacy is often marked by a warm friendship developed through long association. The root word of intimacy is *intima,* referring to the innermost part, such as the intimal lining of the heart. Intimacy might be defined as the condition of knowing and being known at the level of our essential selves. Aspects of disclosure, honesty, and trust are involved, as well.

So how does a casual acquaintance become an intimate friend? Is there a specific moment when the shift occurs? Why do complete strangers suddenly reveal deeply personal aspects of their characters to one another? And why do other people withhold vital information about themselves from their long-term companions? Is there an internal signal that indicates it's all right to trust one another?

Intimacy is not something we can decide to have. We can only discover its presence in the process of everyday living. Intimacy occurs when we share our essential selves, which is not always an intentional or conscious act. It is a look behind the mask of personality, that construction of characteristics we create to function in a complex, impersonal, and demanding society. When we drop our masks with one another, we have a feeling of connection, of being truly *known*. And, although most of us say we want more intimacy in our lives, we regard it with profound ambivalence: we feel attracted to and repelled by it at once. As lovely as it sounds, the reality of intimacy seems somehow dangerous.

The reason for this perceived danger is illustrated dramatically by responses to a simple assignment in my journalkeeping workshops. After the first session, dealing with obstacles to keeping a journal, I ask participants to describe their own personal fears related to journalwriting. The responses—and in over eight years of teaching, I've read hundreds of them—reveal a common conviction.

- ◦ *"I am afraid if I find out who I really am, I'll hate myself."*
- ◦ *"I am afraid that I am unimportant and uninteresting."*
- ◦ *"I fear my lies would become apparent."*
- ◦ *"I fear I have nothing to say."*
- ◦ *"I fear finding out something terrible about myself."*
- ◦ *"I am afraid I will see how shallow and worthless I am."*
- ◦ *"I fear if I listen to myself, there will be nothing to hear."*

How many variations are there to the basic theme, "I'm afraid if I really know myself, I'll hate myself"? If this is a sample of our core beliefs about ourselves, it should come as no surprise that intimate relationships strike fear in our hearts. The myth of self-hatred serves to isolate us from one another and keeps us disconnected from our essential nature. How could I dare reveal my innermost being if I believe there is nothing of value to share? Before I can allow you to know me, I must risk knowing myself.

Exercise: *Mirroring*

As co-author of this book, write a short paragraph introducing yourself. Use third person. (Example: *"Kay Hagan is a writer, teacher, and consultant. She likes reggae music, the ocean, and cats."*)

Now write another paragraph describing yourself to a prospective employer, housemate, lover, or business partner. This time, use first person.

When we are first getting to know someone, we tend to selectively share ourselves, slanting our image toward what we think will be attractive. In the early stages of journalkeeping, our entries may seem stilted and forced. Our fear of discovering "something terrible" about ourselves can keep us on a superficial level, when in actuality, we already know ourselves completely—there are no secret timebombs waiting to explode when we turn our attention to them. Sometimes, we deny or repress our conscious awareness of certain experiences because they are too painful, such as incest or other forms of abuse, and this denial allows us to survive those experiences. But whether or not we consciously remember them, we know these things occurred. An important part of the healing process includes accepting and claiming those powerful experiences that continue to influence us, consciously or not. Although this phase of healing can be painful, it allows us to regain our wholeness, to feel honestly and deeply known in our relationship with self. Our natural condition is one of complete self-knowledge. What we have to work at is bringing that knowledge to consciousness, and this effort brings us into conflict with our conditioning.

The dominant culture of society does not encourage the knowledge of self because that knowledge cultivates creativity, independence, and defiance of authority. Instead, attempts to develop self-awareness meet with charges of being self-centered, selfish, obsessive, or indulgent. We internalize these messages at an early age, and by the time we are adults, the equation of the desire for self-knowledge with selfishness is hard to defy. You may have experienced some difficulty deciding whether or not to purchase this book because of its outright intention to cultivate self-intimacy. Doing the exercises may trigger these messages again, such as "Why are you wasting your time with this stuff?" "What's the point of all this navel-gazing baloney?" "You should be doing something useful." As you hear these negative comments, make a note of them in the margins. Bringing these messages to consciousness will allow you to interact in an intentional manner rather than being influenced by them unconsciously. In Chapter Four, we will focus specifically on our internal voices and how they affect us in everyday life.

As in any intimate relationship, intimacy with self takes time to develop. We must earn our own trust by listening attentively and without judgement, by being available to ourselves with quality time, by attending to our own needs and desires with generosity and patience, and by honoring our evershifting emotions. At this point, it may help to explore your own definition and understanding of intimacy.

Exercise: Wordtrip

Clear your mind, take a breath, and focus on the word *intimacy*. Allow yourself to write down anything that comes to your mind — the sensations, qualities, or characteristics of intimacy. Write quickly, in list form, and don't worry whether or not the words seem to relate directly to intimacy.

Now compare your list with this one, a typical composite of group exercises done in my workshops:

dependency	sharing burdens	pain
willingness	fantasy	illusion
expectations	sexuality	closeness
power	enmeshment	fusion
giving	struggle	maintenance
receiving	anger	love
forgiveness	nurture	hope
birth	dreams	dance
despair	abandonment	sharing
attention	current	caring
trust	experiences	vulnerability
understanding	energy	anxiety
addiction	codependency	joy
risk	pleasure	judgement
fun	acceptance	listening
intensity	revealing	sounding board
scary	terrifying	quietness
comfortable	trapped	commitment
time	priority	sadness
respect	humor	
space	hearing the truth	

When we look at the dramatic contrasts represented on these lists, we begin to understand our ambivalence towards intimacy. The fact is that under the rubric of intimacy, we group all our reactions and responses as well. The same condition that brings joy brings fear. With caring comes vulnerability. When we allow ourselves to become close to someone, and admit our love and desire for them, we may experience loss, rejection, or disappointment. Psychologists describe the phenomenon of "pursuing and distancing" as a pattern in many relationships as people draw closer to intimacy. We know intimacy involves risk. To assume that it has only positive connotations is denying our experience, and creates confusion both internally and externally.

The condition of knowing and being known at the level of our essential selves offers the possibility for connection, with one another and with ourselves. Without intimacy, we remain isolated, shut down, numb, and estranged from life. Knowing the self—gently and respectfully learning who we are, what we want, how we feel, what we think—allows us to bring that knowledge and experience of loving intimacy to our relationships with others. In our self-intimacy, we have the opportunity to create the kind of relationship we most desire. We can treat ourselves the way we want to be treated. Do you know how this would be in your relationship with yourself?

To help answer this question, review the intimacy Wordtrip lists, your own and the composite one. Keep in mind the current relationship you have with yourself and consider how each item on the list relates to it. To explore and assess that relationship further, pose some gentle questions.

○ *"Do I share thoughts and feelings with myself?"*
○ *"Do I nurture myself?"*
○ *"Do I trust myself?"*
○ *"Am I vulnerable with myself?"*
○ *"Do I pleasure myself and have fun with myself?"*
○ *"Do I accept myself? Judge myself?"*
○ *"Do I experience energy and intensity in my relationship with self?"*
○ *"Am I willing to be revealing with myself?"*
○ *"Do I truly listen to my own thoughts?"*
○ *"Do I spend quality time with myself, and do I make this time a priority?"*
○ *"Am I committed to myself?"*
○ *"Do I treat myself with respect?"*
○ *"Do I accept my feelings, whatever they might be?"*

For most of us, it is easier to display these characteristics in our relationships with other people than it is with ourselves. In fact, we rarely consider what the quality of intimacy is in our relationship with self or pay attention to it at all. This invisible presence in our lives is the most enduring and influential relationship we will ever have. And how we treat ourselves affects everything else we do.

Exercise: *Ideal Evening*

Spend a few minutes imagining an ideal evening. It might include a candle-lit dinner, a long bubble bath, a mystery novel, a walk in the moonlight, anything you like. Describe the evening in great detail. After you've completed your description, make a date to share this evening with yourself, and do it! After the evening, record your responses in your journal.

The journal represents a safe space where you can reveal yourself, encounter yourself, and know yourself. It is accessible and private. In the journal, you have the opportunity to express yourself without having to consider the feelings or concerns of anyone else: the opportunity for totally free expression. Our feelings about freedom hold much of the same ambivalence as our feelings towards intimacy. Although we long for it, we may not know what to do when we have it. Journalkeeping offers us the experience of freedom—we can practice being, knowing and loving our essential selves. Eventually, as we experience self-acceptance and self-knowledge in the sacred setting of our journal, it becomes easier to bring this level of openness and expression to our relationships with others.

If we long for intimacy and freedom, and journalkeeping provides us with both, what stops us from doing it?

INNER VIEW

What brings you pleasure?

Fear: 2
Removing Obstacles

ALTHOUGH EXCUSES FOR NOT writing are probably infinite in number and variety, a unifying thread is the tendency to set up unrealistic expectations and unreasonable standards, such as writing every day or using perfect grammar. We create situations where we are disappointed, and we pounce upon the opportunity to say, "See? I've failed again!" We sit back, secure in the knowledge that we've once again predicted our shortcomings, and we put the journal aside. In reality, all we've proven is that we can't meet our own unreasonable standards. As this game disguises deeper fears of becoming intimate with ourselves, and discovering something terrible, it prohibits us from discovering the wealth of personal power offered by self-awareness. The opportunity and challenge of intimacy and freedom will have to wait.

Our conditioning provides each of us with a unique script loaded with such negative comments. While excuses prevent a connection with the essential self, they also reveal where a connection is possible. We create each obstacle from our fears, and when we address them directly, our inhibited energy is released.

The following eight examples are the most common personal obstacles to journalkeeping, and how to transform them.

Physical Form

"I buy these beautiful journals, thinking 'this time I'm really going to do it,' then when I get home, I feel the journal is too pretty to mess up."

What is the right journal? Only you can say. The physical form of your journal, and the pen you use, are the tangible aspects of your relationship—the sensual part, if you will. A journal should attract you and physically please you. The paper can be lined, unlined, or gridmarked according to your preference. If you want to write on both sides of the page, the binding should allow the book to open flat; it might be casebound or spiral. And the paper should be thick enough and of high enough quality to keep from bleeding through or "fuzzing" with the ink.

Why is physical form so important in this relationship of freedom and intimacy? Because there are enough obstacles to journalkeeping without making the journal itself one of them! If you are in any way uncomfortable with the feel of your journal, that feeling will stand in the way of your writing. You want to pave the way to that moment with all the pleasure you can, and unlike many of the other issues discussed in this chapter, physical form is one over which you have complete control.

So have fun exploring stationery stores, office supply houses, and art supply shops searching for just the right journal. Recently, I've returned to a particular kind of spiral notebook, college-ruled, with a soft green "eye-ease" paper. I like the commonness of the book; it is unintimidating and easy to be with. I like to personalize each new volume by putting a photograph, postcard, or image cut from a magazine on the cover to create a visual theme for the journal.

Dallas bookbinder Linda Finnell has taught me some simple binding techniques so I can bind my own journals. It is especially pleasing to choose a special paper for the cover, and delicious text paper for the inside. I have found that on certain occasions, when I am anticipating a particularly eventful phase of my life such as a long journey or a special project, I will create a new journal to honor the phase.

Finding Time

"I could never find time to write in a journal."

Finding time for journalkeeping is exactly that: discovering special pockets of time within your normal routine to spend with yourself. Most of us are busier than we want to be. We have more on our calendars and in our appointment books than we can do. How can we find time for one more thing, especially something like journalkeeping which may never find its way to the top of a to-do list?

The ability to find time is easy to recognize when we look at it in our relationships with other people. Suppose you meet someone at a party or at a friend's house, you have an exciting conversation, and you find yourself wanting to get to know this person. "I'd like to get together soon," you say. "Yes, let's do," your new friend says. Both of you pull out those calendars, crammed to the limit just a moment before, and suddenly as you scan the pages, blocks of time appear, time you never imagined existed. You find a common date and agree to meet. Because you are interested, curious and want to spend time getting to know this person, you find time. It's a magical quality, the elastic, expansive nature of time.

When you begin to view yourself as a fascinating person you want to know better, you may discover those same hidden pockets of time. Some people make dates with themselves. They look ahead in their schedule for the week and pencil themselves in: "On Thursday, I'll have lunch alone, take my journal, and have a good check-in." A particular advantage of this method is that, assured of getting time with yourself, you take mental notes throughout the week of subjects you want to discuss in your journal.

Other people like to designate a special time of day to write, over morning coffee, or just before bed. This helps them incorporate the journal into their routine—whether they choose to spend that time writing, meditating, or just being quiet with themselves. Having a simple ritual helps focus attention: lighting a candle or some incense, unplugging the telephone for a few moments, having a cup of tea.

Keeping your journal with you throughout the day allows

you to take advantage of unexpected waits. I make some of my favorite entries waiting for a delayed dinner companion in a restaurant, or catching an unplanned snack somewhere.

Journalkeeping is quality time spent listening to yourself, getting to know yourself, not another burdensome item on the never-ending to-do list. Writing in your journal is a time of paying attention to yourself, attuning to your deeper voices and concerns. It is not homework, a test, a chore; it is not a dentist appointment or piano practice. It is not a "should."

Regular Entries

"I have absolutely no self-discipline! I could never write every day. I've tried to start a hundred times, but I drift away after a week or so."

Most people assume that they must write every single day to keep a "successful" journal. More than any other issue, this mythical standard undermines journalkeeping for hundreds of otherwise conscientious people. I've had dozens of students over the years begin a workshop by declaring, "This time, I'm going to stick to it! I've paid my money for this workshop, and I'm going to write every single day from now on, because if I don't write every day, what's the point?" Subsequently, by the end of the second or third week of class, they are very discouraged.

I call this the "All-or-Nothing Sabotage" and it's a sure-fire prescription for failure. Writing each and every day is an unrealistic expectation, and it is not a criterion for a successful journal. The journal is not a place of judgement, standards, or competition. Journalkeeping is not a competitive sport. It is a place of freedom, of gentle reflection, a structure that flexes, bends, and shifts as you do, not a rigid prison with a guard ready to rap your knuckles for missing a day, a week, or a month of entries. That's right: you can miss a month or more of writing in your journal and still be a successful journal-keeper.

"Regular entries" are defined by your own desires. As you allow yourself to write as often or as infrequently as you want, you will discover your own pace, a natural, unique cycle that includes times of voracious writing as well as times of silence. An attitude of permissiveness gives you the opportunity to observe what it is that motivates you to write, and you will become more sensitized to your moods. You will have the compulsion to write at different times, but the feeling itself will become familiar. It may be a need to ground your energy or to check in with yourself.

The main issue, once again, is freedom.

As long as you set up journalkeeping as a test of discipline, you will find yourself lacking in commitment. When you allow yourself to experience the freedom and intimacy possible in journalkeeping, you'll discover many different reasons for wanting to write. Making an entry every single day is an empty goal. Charting your course through life is an adventure.

Learn to be kind to yourself: you can write whenever you wish, and you can pause whenever you wish. Regardless of how long it has been since you opened it, your journal need never feel like one more task on your to-do list, but rather a space of welcome, acceptance, and loving attention. Why do we insist on making a chore out of an activity that is healing, nurturing, and accepting? I suspect that most of us are unaccustomed to having a constant healing presence in our lives; it is far more familiar and comfortable to deal with a critical, judgmental voice. In a subtle, profound way, journalkeeping gives us the opportunity to practice loving ourselves.

Silences

"Sometimes I stop writing for weeks."

In context, periods of silence become valuable clues to your natural writing cycle. Sometimes, a silence indicates a particularly busy time or a phase when you are "gestating" on a difficult emotional problem before you are ready to articulate it consciously. A silence might indicate a pause before a creative insight, or a time of denial and avoidance. In context, these quiet times reveal many things.

To observe your silences, I suggest that when you return to

your journal after a significant amount of time (for me it is about ten days), skip a space—at least several lines—leaving a blank area for the silence to "live" in. When you read back over the journal, the space will catch your eye, alerting you to the presence of a silence. Then you can pay particular attention to what preceded and followed the silence, possibly diagnosing the meaning of the silent period.

Appropriate Material

"Nothing I do or think is important enough to write down."

When the painter Georgia O'Keeffe was in her late twenties, she decided that all her paintings and drawings were derivative, done to satisfy someone else. One day, she burned canvases and sketchbooks alike in a great bonfire, declaring "the canvas was the one place in the world where I had absolute freedom, and I was a damn fool not to use it." Starting over with newsprint and canvas, she began to draw the "shapes in [her] head" for which she had seen no model. These images marked the beginning of the work which brought her both personal satisfaction and worldwide fame. When O'Keeffe had the courage to claim her canvas as a place of freedom, she reached a deeper level of creative vision and internal wisdom.

A journal is that canvas, a place of absolute, personal freedom. This freedom from anyone's rules or standards, even your own, may be more intimidating than a strict list of do's and don'ts. By releasing yourself from any expectations or standards, you give yourself permission to write anything at all: a love letter, a fantasy, a whiney complaint, a pack of lies, a diatribe against the state, or the exact same thing you wrote yesterday. You may write about not knowing what you want to write. Everything is appropriate.

The point to remember is that in journalkeeping there is no right or wrong. Anything you record may prove to be a clue to your self-knowledge, even your silences. In the moment, there is no way anyone can discern which thoughts or events will prove to be important, so if you wait for that *important* thought before you begin to write, you may wait for a long time! If you do let yourself write freely, you will discover later on that what seemed insignificant at the time has become amazingly informative and revealing when placed in context and seen with "20/20 hindsight."

I give myself permission to unload my scattered thoughts in the first few minutes of writing—broken phrases, unfinished sentences, and profanity—and I find my real concerns buried under them. In mining for gold, you have to dig through loads of dirt and stone before you get to the glimmering ore; if you don't have the patience to go through the first, you never get to the second. Writing anything, simply writing for the sake of writing, will shift your consciousness to a more intimate realm, and you will begin hearing from a deeper level of awareness. In this way, journalkeeping is similar to meditation. The act of writing is a gesture indicating you are ready to communicate—to listen, transcribe, and converse—with your inner self.

As you become comfortable with a free flow of words, you may choose to expand your journal to include nonverbal entries: drawings or images cut from magazines, favorite snapshots, scribblings, pressed flowers, locks of hair, a leaf, or a feather. Many times these images will inspire you to write even more. The journal is a reflection of the rich, complex, intricate pattern of your life and need not be restricted to words. But the trust that your journal is a place of absolute freedom is fragile and can be shattered easily if privacy is not secured.

Privacy

"I'm terrified someone might read my journal. I would be so ashamed!"

As far as I can tell, the fear of a journal being read is universal. Participants in my classes have fears of mates, lovers, friends, enemies, and especially parents reading their words. "If my mother ever read this!" "If my lover/friend/husband knew what I really felt!" "What if someone reads this after I die?" In one form or another, these fears seem to plague everyone, and with good reason. The experience of having our journals violated is traumatic, especially in childhood. If your private writing was read by a parent when you were a child, you may carry a deep, unnamed fear of anticipated invasion, a fear which keeps you from writing freely and honestly as an adult. If this is the case for you, remember that you are in a position of personal control now, and you can protect yourself from this abuse.

Privacy is essential to journalkeeping and every one of us has a right to it. If you are afraid someone is going to read your journal without your consent, you will censor your entries against that invasion. Instead of enjoying your journal as a place of freedom, you will carry to it the fear of betrayal.

Protect your privacy! Do whatever is necessary to secure your journal as the sacred, private space that it is. Here are some suggestions:

○ *Find a locked drawer, or a hiding place, or purchase a cash drawer with a lock and key or combination for storing your journal.*

○ *Carry it with you everywhere. (This also encourages you to write more spontaneously!)*

○ *Write a warning on the frontispiece of each journal: "For my eyes only. Anyone reading this journal without permission does so at their own risk, and must take responsibility for that invasion."*

Invasion

"My last lover read my journal and it caused a horrible fight. Why would anyone do such a thing?"

The temptation to read someone's journal can be difficult to overcome. For a few years in my early twenties, I was married to a serious young man with whom I had a wonderful friendship. As we assumed the roles of husband and wife, we had difficulty conforming to the societal responsibilities associated with them. He became cold and withdrawn, and I was convinced that my wifely duties included probing his thoughts and feelings. We were both avid journalkeepers, and after a year or more of his chronic distancing, I felt compelled to read his journal. I sincerely believed that it would help me understand the things he could not express to me but could write in the journal, and that this would help me make the marriage work. So I read them. I read them in a fever, over months, convinced that I would find the reasons for his withdrawal. I did find evidence of his sadness and confusion, but I did not find the answers to my questions. By then, I realized I had betrayed him in a way I could never confess. I could not even use the "knowledge" I had gained for then he would know of my betrayal. In an effort to mend the marriage, I essentially contributed to the barriers between us. Undoubtedly, it was one of the worst feelings I've ever had.

I share this story for two reasons. First, for everyone who ever wanted to read another's journal or succumbed to that temptation, I want you to know you are not alone. Second, I want to illustrate emphatically what a powerful influence journalkeeping can have on relationships with others. In your intimate relationships, especially when you are living with others either as partners or housemates, it is natural to be concerned with communication. Their curiosity about what you are writing will be in direct proportion to the quality of communication in the relationship. If you are going through a time of distancing or confusion (which generally inspires more journal entries), they may be wondering, "What are you telling the journal that you are not telling me? What are you writing about me?" At difficult points like this, reading someone's journal seems infinitely easier than discussing our insecurities face to face. I am not condoning this attitude; I am simply acknowledging a probability based on personal experience.

Writing your personal thoughts, observations, dreams, fears, and opinions in your private journal is not and can never be wrong. But reading another's private writings without permission is an act of violation and betrayal. If someone reads your journal, they are committing an act of invasion. At the moment when they confront you, you may have a tendency to feel ashamed or guilty because what they have read may have hurt or angered them. But the reverse is also true: their act of invasion and violation has hurt you. You have the right to be angry, and you need not discuss anything that they read in your journal. What you write in your journal is yours. It is your private, sacred space. You have no obligation to tell the truth, to tell the whole story, or to shield anyone from what is written in your journal. The violator's act of betrayal will damage the relationship far more than anything they discover. While this may not lessen your fears, understanding the nature of this act can clarify the moment when and if it occurs.

If you are concerned about your intimates reading your journal, consider talking to them. Explain that you are developing an intimacy with yourself and you need to feel safe as you record this journal. Assure them your writing is not an act of distancing from them, but an act of choosing yourself. Suggest that their curiosity is natural and is not wrong; but, if they act on that curiosity, they will have betrayed and hurt you. Ask that if they find themselves tempted to read your journal, to please come and tell you. At that time you can make the decision to find something in it to share with them, or you can examine the relationship to find what communication problems have contributed to this temptation.

If you are concerned about your journals being read after you die, discuss your fear with a trusted friend. Make an agreement that in the event of your death, the friend will immediately locate your journals and destroy or secure them according to your wishes.

Examine your needs and fears around invasion and privacy, and honor these feelings by creating an environment of safety and security around your journalkeeping. Without it, you will not be willing to hear at the deepest level of your being or write with the honesty that will lead you to your heart's wisdom. We all have a right to our privacy, especially when we are doing the tender work of self-reflection.

Exercise: *Safe Space*

In the next few days, observe your feelings and needs concerning privacy and determine what measures you want to take to secure your journal as a safe space for you. The desire for privacy is not a precious adolescent attitude, but an essential element of nurture and protection.

Censoring

"I just put down superficial stuff. . . . I can't make myself be really honest. I censor myself."

When the external environment has become safe, the internal one may still resist. While writing freely you may find that you are knowingly excluding information, or shaping the flow to do something else. What is actually happening is that you are silencing your own voice. This is accomplished through internal censoring.

Censors are internal sentries that guard information and keep it from coming to consciousness. Censors compartmentalize certain information—tender memories, painful fears, scary dreams, unnecessary or untimely details, or even powerful images of self-love that our conditioning armors against entering our awareness. The reasons for this withholding of information are usually unclear and unstated. The evidence surfaces only when the censor acts. The information held back by internal censors are secrets you are keeping from yourself.

Internal censors can come in many forms. Most often, they will surface in self-critical remarks at the moment of writing: "Your writing is so clumsy, why do you even bother?" "Do you think this is really important enough to write down?" "It didn't happen exactly this way." The internal editor serves the purpose of censoring quite efficiently, whether intentionally or not. A quality controller, this editor insists on high literary style and complete sentences—as well as lovely handwriting.

As you begin to bring these self-critical remarks into audible consciousness, you can banish them, reminding yourself that the journal is your freedom space where you can write anything you wish, in any form you wish.

Censors can appear also as decoys, distractions, or saboteurs. Sometimes I'll be writing along and suddenly think, "I must go do the dishes piled up in the sink!" Without making a conscious decision I am halfway through the dishes before I realize, "What am I doing? I was writing in my journal!" I will go back and see that, more often than not, I jumped up in mid-sentence, mid-word, just as I was getting into a sensitive subject. The compelling task of the dishes was a censor in disguise.

However, censoring is not necessarily negative. A few years ago, after challenging myself to write without censoring at all, I soon realized that if I removed all the censors at once, the barrage of information would be emotionally overwhelming. Censors are performing an important and sensitive job. Consciously used, they are powerful allies. The same censor whose job it is to withhold information can be transformed into a *sensor*, whose function is to report information. The oil sensor in a car is designed to monitor constantly to keep you apprised of the current level of oil. In the same way, a *censor* monitors what is happening, but does not divulge the information. A censor can become a sensor as soon as you decide to probe past the guard at the door. The sensor will reveal a vast storehouse of information to you, giving you the opportunity to "re-view" it.

Here is an example of the censor/sensor transformation: some years ago, I noticed I began to block whenever I wrote about my younger brother. My conscious impression of my relationship with him was one of admiration, sweetness, and awe—he is seven years younger than me and quite an adventurer. I was troubled by my censoring but unwilling to explore it further until I began to have a series of vivid and disconcerting dreams about him. The information was nudging its way to the surface, past the censors, through my dreams. When I felt emotionally strong enough, I decided to probe my memory and ask myself some specific questions about my feelings. I used my journal to record my recollections.

What I discovered led me on a long journey in re-viewing my relationship with my brother. I recalled the earliest days of his life, and realized that laced in my admiration of his adventureousness was a great deal of jealousy, and I discovered plenty of sibling rivalry among the memories of our childhood. I had successfully masked those feelings from myself for years by censoring them, because they seemed inappropriate. When I was ready to accept that part of myself, it was waiting for me. The censoring itself had caught my conscious attention and gave me the important clue necessary to work through my denial.

So at first, instead of banishing your censors, simply begin to observe when and how they work. One way to do this is to notice as you are writing. When you begin to censor, put a small *c* in the margin as a code. Do not stop the flow of your writing or attempt to challenge the censor's authority for the moment. After a period of using this technique, you will have visual reference of your censoring pattern. You will be able to look at the issues and subjects that triggered the censoring, and the thoughts you held back will become clearer. In a way, this method illuminates the censor's secrets in reverse. It is a way to make friends with your censors, getting to know those parts of yourself that are taking responsibility for information control. The goal is to make them visible, to learn more about the information that is being withheld, and to discover the secrets you are keeping from yourself.

In any intimacy, the telling of secrets marks an important passage and deepening of the relationship. Sometimes the secrets are from our past; for example, early in a relationship I have often felt hesitant to reveal my birth family's problems with alcoholism. Another form of secret is a held feeling, a thought or emotion we have but do not express, perhaps because it is painful or scary to share. In order to disclose any secrets, however, we want to be reasonably certain our intimate will hear us with compassion, acceptance, and a willingness to process any conflict that might arise.

In self-intimacy, we want to make sure that we are willing to treat ourselves with a similar respect, and without judgement, before we raise to consciousness feelings and memories that are painful or scary. We must earn our own trust just as we must earn a friend's. If you feel yourself lapsing into self-criticism, judgement, or berating as you write, pause for a moment and take a breath. Give yourself support for the risk you are taking and spend a few minutes writing affirmations: "I accept myself just as I am," or "I am eager to know all the parts of my diverse experience," or "I welcome self-knowledge for the wisdom it brings." Treat yourself as you would want a lover, friend, or relative to treat you in a similar situation.

Exercise: *Obstacle/Inspiration*

Each obstacle to journalkeeping disguises an inspiration. Spend a few minutes here thinking over your own blocks to journalkeeping and write them down. Consider how you can free yourself from each fear or block, and write a statement of affirmation about it. As you continue through the book, you may discover other obstacles that surface when you begin to go deeper into yourself; when you do, return to this space and add them to your list. Specifically naming them will give you guidance on how to transform that blocked energy into a free, flowing, personal conversation.

Now that our obstacles are cleared, we can start to learn more about ourselves, beginning with our memories.

INNER VIEW

When was the last time you felt afraid? Describe the circumstances and what happened.

INNER VIEW

If you could change one thing about yourself, what would
it be and why?

Memory: *3* Sharing the Past

*M*EMORY IS OUR AUTOBIOGRAPHY, constantly being written and revised—a living, breathing document we record and hold in our minds. It is a selective interpretation of our personal history that influences us in each moment as we make our daily decisions. Our memories are highly personalized versions of the truth of our past experiences. To become familiar with our memories—their selectivity, biases, embellishments, and symbolism—enables us to deepen our self-intimacy, to avoid illusion and denial, and to make more empowering decisions. But the trust we need to share our memories freely in a relationship must be present in our self-intimacy as well.

Friendships are built on shared experiences, some of which are direct and mutual, while others are shared vicariously with one friend relating a story to another. As we feel closer to each other, we begin to share the stories of our past often comparing similar moments—how we felt when a parent died, or when we first saw the ocean, or when we first made love. Feeling our trust build, we reach into our memories and pull out our personal history, sharing as much as we dare. An intimacy can deepen quickly by the sharing of memories, for when we share stories of our past, we are revealing more than facts. We reveal how we feel about ourselves, what inspires us and provides meaning, as well as what haunts us. If we experience judgement, criticism, rejection, or ridicule when we reveal ourselves to someone, we are unlikely to do it again.

In the same way, working with personal memories calls for sensitivity and compassion in your intimacy with self. Having established the journal as a place of freedom, you can recount your memories in safety, exploring your unique interpretations of the past and how it affects your current outlook.

This chapter covers the influence and layers of memory, how it relates to journalkeeping, and the Memory Probe, a tool designed for the safe and easy retrieval of specific memory points.

The power of memory's influence comes from three aspects: selectivity, symbolism, and repetition. While I have often heard that our brains record everything we perceive, I have found that I cannot recall everything at will. Instead, when I reach into the past to pull out a certain experience, I receive a carefully selected version of that event. The more distant the memory, the more selective the version, but even short-term memories have gone through the selection process. This edited version of the past is part truth, part fiction—an unintended distortion of what "really" happened. Because of this selection process, our memories are actually symbolic representations of our experiences, and as we recall them again and again over time, we reinforce the message of this symbolic story as if it were the truth. Here's an example.

Recently, I spent two weeks in the mountains working on the manuscript for this book. I was alone, and I worked every morning and afternoon for several hours, remembering what my chiropractor had advised about stretching my neck and shoulders every half-hour. I came up with some great new material, though I knew I would have to cut it down a bit. And I indulged myself with childhood treats to help ease the intensity. I ate what I craved and took nature walks—one day I saw a beaver and a hummingbird. It was quite the perfect writing retreat.

But when I returned to my city routine, literally within hours I heard myself giving this description of my "perfect writing retreat": "It was not as productive as I'd hoped. I seemed to have a limited concentration span, and the new chapter dragged on and on. I kept getting up from the keyboard and wandering around, eating chocolate chip cookies and drinking raspberry tea, staring out the window like a zombie. I finally got through the draft, but it was like pulling teeth!"

The facts of both versions are essentially true. No facts are left out or twisted, yet one recollection radiates with excitement and affirmation while the other reeks of negative criticism, judgement, perfectionism, and self-hatred. By the time I had repeated my negative version of the retreat to several friends, I managed to convince myself that I had squandered the time. I felt I had let myself down, and that I had failed. *How* we remember is as important as *what* we remember, and this is the power of memory's symbolism.

How do we decide what to recall and what to forget? By recording your memories, both short and long term, in your journal, you create a document that allows you to explore the selection process, to reveal the symbols created by your memory, and to understand more clearly how your memories may be reinforcing particular images and messages in the present moment, carrying them into the future.

Much of what we write in our journals comes from memory. I recall a distressing conversation from earlier in the week, describe it in the journal, then record my feelings, both past and present. The longer I wait to register this information—the longer I hold it in my mind without recording it—the less vivid and more selective the written version will be. We are constantly adding layers to our memories, like the rings of a tree trunk.

I have defined four layers of memory to emphasize its different qualities and uses in relation to journalwork. Here is a brief definition of each, followed by more detailed explanations.

1. *Immediate Present.* The present moment give or take three days; the layer that yields the most vivid, undistorted detail.

2. *Recurring Memories.* A handful of "golden oldies" that return spontaneously, often attached to powerful moments of decision or sentiment.

3. *Easily Accessible.* The information stored just below the surface of consciousness that can be retrieved easily but does not intrude on the present moment.

4. *Fugitive Information.* The memories "lost in the system" of the mind, repressed, hidden, or stored in the body, retrievable with care and intention.

The *immediate present* has particular importance for journalkeeping as it affords the most complete recall of detail with the least amount of selection. As the outer layer of the tree trunk, the immediate present is not yet covered by other impressions and can provide a more accurate rendering of an experience with all its complexities of emotion, thought, and sensation. My own recall of the immediate present lasts only about three days. After that, the selection process begins in earnest, and my recollections are dimmed and influenced by an overlay of more recent impressions and thoughts. To obtain an "eyewitness" quality of memory, make a journal entry within three days of an event. You can examine the memory's selection process in progress by trying the following exercise.

Exercise: *Hindsight*

Make a journal entry immediately after an event. Two weeks later, without reviewing your former entry, make another entry recalling the event. Compare the two and notice the selection process.

Recurring memories have a shimmering quality about the images, and generally the memory is just that: a single image. Most of my recurring memories come from before the age of twelve and are often provoked by a sensory experience—the aroma of baking bread, the sight of the first red autumn leaf, the feel of sand under my feet. Usually just a handful, these memories sometimes recur as dream symbols or settings and have a mesmerizing effect.

Sometimes recurring memories are moments of decisions made in childhood and carried forward, unexamined, into adult life. Here is an example from a workshop participant.

> One afternoon when I was about nine years old, I remember walking down the stairs, into the family room. There had been some sort of altercation there. I believe I had been scolded and I escaped to my room for a while. When I was about to rejoin the family, I remember pausing on the stairway, my hand on the banister. I said to myself, "I will not cry." I know I didn't mean, "I will never cry again" but I am thirty-five years old, and I have not cried since that moment. I am still working on allowing myself to cry. Somehow, I made a decision in an instant that has stayed with me all these years.

Not every recurring memory will be attached to such a powerful decision, but it is intriguing to explore the reasons why a memory returns. The first step in working with these recurring memories is noticing them. As you have these recurring images, note them briefly in your journal. When you are ready to explore past the superficial layer of the image, you can set aside a special time to examine it for deeper significance in a journal exercise.

Easily accessible memories make up the vast reservoir of stored information that is ready to be tapped but does not invade daily consciousness. Usually, when you probe into a memory fragment, an amazing amount of detail will emerge. "Trip to Mexico, 1977" becomes the smell of gardenias, the pungency of pernod, devil whistles, and whitefish from the high lake of Patzquaro.

Fugitive information is a term I borrowed from the computer world, describing information that has become lost in the system. In a computer, this data does not respond to programming and will appear on the screen at random, in the middle of something entirely unrelated. Then it will disappear, refusing to be invoked by the determined effort of the most earnest hacker. I use the term to describe memories that are repressed, forgotten, hidden, dreams not written down, or brilliant ideas that slipped away from consciousness because I didn't pay attention to them. Fugitive information differs from recurring memories in that it usually comes from a more contemporary time rather than the distant past.

Some fugitive information appears "in my neck," the experiences I store in my body as tension and rigidity until the accumulated pain demands healing, or until my body numbs to the stress and I "forget" about it. A personal example comes from an unresolved conflict with a friend; I see her face, tense and somber, during our last conversation some years ago. It returns to me less frequently now, but I will see it at the oddest of times, and then it will slip away. Because I have tender feelings about the friendship, I try to "forget" our conflict. But the fugitive information is alive and well. These renegade images are flickering through my memory, waiting for a safe haven to call them in. After all, a fugitive is one who is seeking refuge, fleeing from danger or threat. These memories are accessible if we clear our attitude of judgement and listen deeply and patiently.

To work effectively and safely, we must respect the many-layered depth of our memory, as well as the tenderness we may encounter and the emotions we may stir. The next section offers a tool especially designed for this work.

The Memory Probe

Imagine yourself as an archaeologist out in the field on an elaborate dig for remnants of an ancient era. The sole purpose of this expedition is to find likely specimens of dinosaur bones. You will not be able to certify their age or authenticity until you return to the lab, but you can accumulate large amounts of potential specimens. While in the field, you do not stop to ponder whether or not what you have just exhumed is dinosaur or cow; you return to the dig and continue searching. And so it is with your memories. The Memory Probe is the dig.

The Memory Probe is a sequence of steps that helps capture memories with the broadest range of detail and the least amount of self-criticism. Its purpose is to recover information from the past in order to record it in your journal. The technique creates an attitude encouraging the unimpeded flow of memory in an environment free of judgement.

There are seven steps in the Memory Probe. Following the sequence is important for establishing trust in yourself.

1. *Set up your environment with safety, space, and adequate time.*

This kind of journalwork is meditative. You are delving deeply into your psyche to retrieve information, some of which could be painful, surprising, or delightful. You must create a space that honors this work. As the archaeologist carefully ropes off the area of the dig to protect it from unwitting trespassers, you can protect yourself from interruption by unplugging your phone or putting a "do not disturb" sign on your door. Choose a time when you can spend at least an hour on the exercise. You will ask yourself to open up and become vulnerable, so you don't want to attempt a Memory Probe when you must be somewhere else in fifteen minutes. Remember the comparison to a relationship with a friend, and imagine how you would feel if you were in the midst of confiding the tender memory of your first real love affair, and your friend glanced away, started, and left abruptly. By reserving adequate time for your Memory Probe, you are honoring the risk-taking aspect of self-intimacy. You need time to open up your memory, time to explore, and time to emerge from the past and rest before you reenter the present.

2. *Clear your attitude—suspend judgement.*

Have you ever thought back to an early experience and said to yourself, "If only I knew then what I know now." When you do a Memory Probe, you have the opportunity to go back and review a previous moment with all the experience and wisdom you've gained in the meantime. Unfortunately, I've found that many of us have a nearly irresistible tendency to use this opportunity to judge ourselves with extreme harshness. "How could I have been so stupid?" our internal critic scolds. "Why in the world did I make that decision? Couldn't I see what was happening? It's so obvious!" This negative self-talk and inappropriate analysis will send your memories scurrying back to the depths of consciousness and leave you feeling hurt.

By suspending judgement at the outset of your Memory Probe, you will remind your internal critic that her or his place is in the lab, not in the field. As the archaeologist, you approach the task of analysis only *after* you've gathered all the information you need from the past. There is a time and place when our judgmental faculties are effective and appropriate.

When your memories are flowing onto the page, you may make profound and stirring connections because you are experiencing them again, within the context of your accumulated knowledge. When this occurs, I suggest that you affirm and accept the insight, making a brief notation about it as you continue to probe into the breadth and scope of the memory. Making connections is one of the vital and precious riches of journalkeeping, that wonderful feeling of "Aha! *Now* I understand!" While making connections resembles analysis, it comes from an intuitive level and feels less like figuring it out and more like a resonance with the heart.

3. *In your imagination, build an observation point.*

Some of us fear that if we visit certain parts of our past, we will get trapped there, or that the memories will overwhelm us. This fear is quite common, and I've found that a simple mental image can help ease it. Imagine you are standing at a vantage point where you can safely observe the memory. Make an agreement with yourself that you will return to the present whenever you wish. This will assure your inner self that there are guidelines and boundaries to this exploratory venture.

Any sort of image will do as long as you are establishing a firm grounding in the present and a trust in your power to return to it. One image I've used is a safely railed precipice jutting out over a vast panorama—the continental divide, a huge canyon, or green rolling fields. From the precipice, I can see the entire chronology of my life. With binoculars, I focus on the particular area of interest. From that place, I am safe. I know I am grounded in the present, and I am choosing to review a memory. My journal is my tangible anchor, a tether to the present that connects me to my safe space. I can return to the present at any time. When you have formed your observation point, trust yourself, trust your feelings, allow the memories to come, and let the words flow.

4. *Choose a memory and tug at it.*

If you are probing a single image, begin by describing it as precisely as possible. Allow yourself to free-associate as the details surface, and don't be concerned with accuracy or facts. If you find yourself blanking, fill in the gaps with your imagination. If you are probing a certain age or a time period and do not have a specific memory point to describe, ask yourself gentle questions that will tug at the thread of memory. For example, over a period of several years, I used this technique to probe into age eleven in my childhood, about which I seemed to draw a complete blank. With no specific memory for a beginning point, I conducted a slow and tender interview: "What were my favorite clothes? Did I have a best friend? What grade was I in? Did I like particular foods? Did I have a favorite or hated teacher? Was I taking piano or dancing lessons? Did my family take a summer vacation? How old were my siblings?" The answers began to form a portrait of me at the age of eleven.

5. *Let the memory flow onto the page.*

You could think of a Memory Probe as if you have gone to the video store and selected a movie. Let the tape roll and watch the story! You will be taking notes on what you see and hear — and unlike a video, you'll be able to smell, taste, touch, and feel as well. Resist the impulse to ponder over certain events, and encourage yourself to keep the movie rolling. The momentum of the memory is important — you are trying to recover elusive elements hidden deep in your mind. Once the memories begin to come to consciousness, you want to keep them coming. Breathe, relax, and observe.

6. *Return to the present.*

When you have recorded as much as you wish, take a few moments to tune in to the present moment. Notice your surroundings, remind yourself that you are the age you are, in the place where you are, and that you have returned to the present, just as you said you would. Thank your inner self for helping recover these precious memories.

7. *Physically ground yourself before moving to another activity.*

I discovered the need for this step by error. After a memory probe, or other deep journalwork, I would hop up and go to work, pick up a friend for dinner, or make a phone call. Only a few minutes into the next activity, I would experience a dizzy disorientation — a part of me was still lost in the deep recesses of my memory, reluctant to return to the present hubbub of tasks and relationships. What I suggest is to physically ground yourself: drink a glass of water, eat a snack, take a shower or bath, change clothes — do something physical to ground yourself in your body. The energy you create and draw upon to do internal work takes you out of your body and into your intuitive, spiritual realm. By grounding that energy back into the earth and your body, you will feel rooted and revitalized by your experience, rather than "spaced out."

Our past experiences live on in our memories, but they can also take the form of internal voices that influence our behavior and feelings in the present moment. Take the Memory Probe with you into the next chapter as we turn up the volume on those voices; you may find it useful.

INNER VIEW

Find several snapshots of yourself as a child at different ages; as an infant, at seven, at twelve, and as a teenager. Attach them to the workbook, writing a short caption under each one. When you can set up the environment, choose one of them and do a Memory Probe.

INNER VIEW

What event has caused the most dramatic change in your life? Why?

Internal Voices: Sharing the Essential Self

A FEW WEEKS OR MONTHS into a new relationship, we drop our vigilant "best foot forward" and begin acting "normal." That is, instead of thinking first about what our beloved wants to hear, we simply say what's on our minds. The censorship and performance of infatuation drift away and we relax into our true selves. With this truth comes what is sometimes called old baggage—those beliefs and attitudes created in past relationships that we carry forward, whether or not they are applicable to our new intimacies. This is often a disturbing phase. We might sigh and say, "the honeymoon is over" as we encounter our first conflicts and disagreements. But when we get through them and see that the relationship survives, we experience the real beginning of trust.

In your intimacy with self, this old baggage surfaces in the form of internal voices. These are not voices from outside your head, but voices from within yourself—the continuous internal conversation you carry on in the process of living. Decision-making takes place through debate and consultation among these different inner voices. Much of this discussion occurs unconsciously, just as many of our decisions are made without a deliberate, considered choice. While you may not be consciously aware of this inner dialogue, I can assure you it exists and is a valuable resource for self-understanding.

Our internal voices have many sources: childhood experiences, daily interactions in the world, repetitive programming such as commercials and advertisements—all aspects of our conditioning that tell us (directly and indirectly) how we are expected to behave. These voices rarely come to a unanimous agreement. For many of us, the predominant and most insistent voices of our internal dialogues tend to be judgemental and analytical, but there are others which come from deeper levels—those of the essential self, such as intuition, emotion, spirituality, and desire. In her book *Talking to Yourself,* Pamela Butler draws a distinction between the voices of the "imposed" self and those of the "intrinsic" self. Because these positive voices receive little affirmation in our culture, they are often drowned out by the others. If we do hear them, we learn to ignore or deny them.

Since many internal voices are an extension of our conditioning, they play a major role in determining our behavior. Whether or not you consciously hear these voices, they are influencing you. Over time, by trusting your own loving attention as much as you would an intimate friend's, journalkeeping will allow you to bring the voices to consciousness as you freely record your everyday activities, thoughts and feelings. You will discover that you can survive inner conflicts and learn ways to negotiate with yourself to reach resolution.

The journalwork in this chapter is designed to help you tune in to your internal voices and use your knowledge of them to deepen your self-intimacy. This chapter will cover listening deeply, naming the voices, tracing the source of a voice, challenging the authority of outdated voices, and tuning in to the voice of your essential self.

One of the gifts of intimacy is listening. When a dear friend spends hours listening to me describe a confusion, often she will offer little or no comment. She simply listens. Confident of being heard, I open up to her supportive, loving ear, and I hear myself more clearly.

Like the attentiveness of a friend, journalwriting encourages you to listen to yourself, an integral part of intimacy. You sit down, open the journal, pick up the pen, and listen. As you wait for the impulse to write, you may hear a cacophony of voices vying for your attention, or you may hear silence. Each time you write, you affirm and strengthen the skill of inner listening. Journalkeeping creates a space in your life to still your external activities so your internal voices can come to consciousness.

You may have a desire to censor voices, not recording those you consider unimportant, uninteresting, unflattering, or unacceptable. You'll find, however, that just as in a relationship with another person, you must be able to accept your whole self in order to develop trust. When you risk being honest in your journal, sharing even those things about which you feel the most reluctant, you create the opportunity to experience self-acceptance.

Here's a dialogue between two inner voices I recorded in my journal when I was avoiding working on this chapter. I felt frustrated and angry at myself, and I had been fussing with my editor over revisions, so I decided to try tuning into the resistance and have a conversation with the unfinished manuscript.

Kay: I dread working on you because you're so stubborn, you won't come out.

Book: I've come out already! You keep changing your expectations.

Kay: I want you to be perfect. I want you to be clear, simple, and well-organized.

Book: I'm trying. Don't criticize me! All you have to do is listen and copy what I say. Just walk what you talk: do what you're telling the readers to do!

Kay: Hmmm. I keep wondering if it's simpler than I think.

Book: It is. It's so simple you keep missing it. Don't let your editor's criticism distract you. That's her job; yours is to write, not edit. Remember: you don't have to take her suggestions if you don't want to. Just keep writing.

Kay: I'm resisting this chapter because I am disappointed that it's so disorganized. I thought the last version was so good, so nearly done.

Book: I'm evolving. What you've done has gotten you this far. And it **is** good work. I'm just different than what you imagined. I'm eager to be with you in my physical form. I keep visiting you in images so you won't get discouraged. Things will get easier now. Keep working!

Kay: Thanks. I feel comforted. The stomach tension is easing. Sometimes, I forget you love me and I love you.

What I faced in this dialogue was my perfectionism. I so wanted to be perfect that I was blocking the book's evolution. The voice of my essential self, in this case represented by the book, was a gentle and loving reminder that as I move toward completion of any creative project, I must allow myself to move through the process without harsh judgement.

Here are some suggestions for recording internal voices.

1. *Write whatever you hear.* The first few layers of your internal conversations may seem worthless, such as "I don't know what to write about," "I'm bored with myself," "Nothing comes to mind right away." When these voices are acknowledged, they will stop competing for your attention. Recording this chatter usually clears the way for deeper voices, those of support, nurture, self-worth, and insight.

2. *Do not judge the value of what you are writing.* If you hear your internal editor, write down what she or he is saying. "This sounds just like what you wrote yesterday." "These aren't complete sentences." "Your handwriting is terrible." Then remind yourself (and your editor!) that your journal is a place of absolute freedom, and continue to write.

3. *Think of yourself as an attentive, loving friend.* Just as you want your friends to be open and honest with you, treat yourself with the same respect and trust. Your journal is evidence of your desire to know yourself as a whole, complex, everchanging person. Experiment with trusting the truth of this desire by writing freely.

Once you become familiar with your internal voices, the patterns they represent will become apparent, and you can try identifying them by name. Naming exerts a gentle control. When you name something, you recognize it—from then on. In general, if you find yourself wrestling with ambiguity, confusion, or frustration in your journal, ask yourself to give the feeling a name, and try using images. Do you feel lost at sea? Like you don't have a handle on the problem? Like your tasks are burying you? Give the feeling a personality or a picture. These analogies will help define the vague feelings that can inhibit you. As long as you can't name it, the feeling has power over you.

When you use the technique of naming with your internal voices, you are beginning to recognize patterns in their interplay. Many of the voices imposed by conditioning are quite scripted: they say the same things in many different ways. A certain voice represents a set of concerns or a belief, and it will be triggered by the same kinds of situations.

The first one I could name was "Mother." It was she who instructed me to do the dishes before I wrote in my journal. Although I realized quickly that the voice I identified as Mother had little relation to my actual mother in terms of current priorities and values, the tone and attitude was definitely hers. And my obedience to that voice was as automatic as when I was five. I found that after naming the voice, I could distinguish it easily and immediately. I began to pause when I heard it, and to question it before or instead of obeying it. As I continued to record it in my journal, I observed both in my entries and in my daily patterns how I responded to the voice, what situations triggered it, what kind of logic it used to influence me, how it got my attention, what its motives and preferences were, and what would make it be quiet. In other words, I began to examine the relationship I had with my Mother voice, and I learned I could challenge my unconscious habit of automatic obedience.

When you give a voice a name and a personality, you can explore the complex interrelationships of your internal selves. The more you know about each aspect, the better you can understand the dynamics of your decision-making process, and how you construct your self-image, which is a composite of the parts of yourself represented by your internal voices. Your journal is the ideal place for this exploration, in safety and at your own speed.

Here are some examples of internal voices discovered and named by workshop participants through the years.

○ *Miss Never Enough* is never satisfied.
○ *Susie Stopwatch* takes pains to time every task.
○ *The Best Little Boy* is always tidy even when his mind runs wild.
○ *The Golden Baby* believes you were born to be happy.
○ *The Cheerleader* gives pep talks when times are rough.
○ *The Accusing Finger* is always ready to assign blame.
○ *Cool Hand Luke* keeps emotions in check.
○ *Ms. Fix-it* is always ready to rescue, and let you know it.

Exercise: Naming Voices

Take a few moments to check in with yourself now, and listen to the current group of voices that are in your head, vying for your attention. Try to name one or two. You may want to write down part of their script, and recall when you hear them the most often.

Tracing a Voice to Its Source

After identifying a specific voice, you can begin to explore it, collecting information about it as you do your journalwork. At first, the most important thing is to allow the voice to operate as usual: don't try to stop it or change it. This is the observation period. You want to understand as much as possible about how the voice operates in your normal decision-making process. Tracing the source of a voice involves a process of intentional listening and personal research. Here is a series of steps to follow.

1. *Identify which voice you want to explore.* Choose one that you have been able to distinguish several times or more.

2. *Name it.* Use a short, descriptive term, or an actual name that carries an appropriate feeling.

3. *Listen.* As you write in your journal, record exactly what it says and how other parts of you respond. Don't try to change or stop the voice. Just document its script.

4. *Gather information.* Become familiar with all aspects of the voice's patterns, when and where it speaks up, and how it relates to other voices. Pay attention to its habits. Do this for several weeks, noting what you find in your journal.

5. *Reach into the past.* In a Memory Probe, try to recall when you first heard it to locate the origin of the voice. Recall the particular details of that phase of your life. What were the functions and purposes of the voice at that time?

6. *Compare and get current.* What are the qualities of your current environment? How is it similar to or different from the origination point of your voice? Do you still need the kind of advice the voice is giving you? What other functions could this part of you perform that would be helpful today?

The example of "Little Miss Perfect" shows how this process works.

Little Miss Perfect: A Case History

Some years ago, I named a voice Little Miss Perfect. She was arrogant, self-righteous, and—of course—perfect. She expected perfection from everyone, especially me. I discovered her everywhere: on the job, at home alone, and in my intimacies. I found that after the Mother voice, Little Miss Perfect really ran my life. I decided I needed to know more about her.

I began to pay close attention to her. I scanned my current and past journals listening for her voice there and in my conversations with others. I did research on her habits: what is her agenda? Her likes and dislikes? Where does she like to hang out? What situations trigger her?

I found her very active on the job. I saw that she made me an extremely good employee: super-responsible, a "responsibility magnet." She was self-righteous and had a strong tendency for martyrdom. But there was a positive side to her: super-organized, practical, analytical, and she had fantastic foresight. Little Miss Perfect was a planner and strategist, and I liked these parts of her.

But I noticed that in my intimacies, she was a disaster. Affairs of the heart can't be organized, and certainly not with the degree of perfection upon which Little Miss Perfect insisted. She was a scorekeeper in relationships: argumentative, always right, judgmental, relentlessly critical, and vicious in fights. Although she was extremely loyal, she expected an impossible ideal from her intimates and was often disappointed in their lack of integrity—never quite up to her high standards. I heard a secret superiority edging her tone. As I had the courage to face this part of myself, I wondered how anyone had dared to get close to me.

After getting Little Miss Perfect's profile, my first reaction was, "I must get rid of her!" I discovered that this was not an easy or entirely desirable task. I felt she had always been a part of me; but, when I probed back into my memory, I wondered if my first experiences with her had come in college. This seemed likely: I was working my way through school and there were hard times both financially and emotionally in my family. I could see that the very adult tone of Little Miss Perfect would have been a survival mechanism to make a transition to being on my own. The organizational, practical, purposeful qualities encouraged by the voice would have been very helpful to figure out how to get through college. For some months, I worked with this premise, observing my behavior and modifying my habits to pull Little Miss Perfect out of my emotional relationships, while continuing to examine her through my journals.

Concurrently, I was working with issues stemming from having alcoholism in my family, and I had begun to identify many habits begun in a family system that included substance addiction and unhealthy emotional patterns. I decided to visit my mother to do some personal research, but I didn't want to trigger a confrontational scene. I only wanted to hear some family stories. I decided to go through the family photograph album with her as a setting for sharing memories that would be neutral and loving. (This technique is an excellent adjunct to Memory Probes.)

As we went through the photos, I prompted certain stories, and the afternoon was comfortable, helpful, and enjoyable. As we got to the bottom of the box of albums, Mom and I came to the formal portraits of the children at different ages. Suddenly, looking at a photo of myself at six years old, I felt a chill in my heart: I saw her, every Toni-curl in place, barrettes smartly fastened, organdy Sunday-school dress neatly ironed —Little Miss Perfect! My young face held the tension of fearlessness and fierceness I recognized. She looked determined and coldly calculating—lips pursed in a firm smile, arrogant, bold, challenging, perfect. I was shocked that she was so young, but the resonance I felt in my heart was undeniable. Little Miss Perfect was a part of my personality that was in full force when I was six years old, and probably earlier.

I remembered being the child with the stubborn streak, hard-headed, and sullen. I was the child who would talk back to her parents, ask questions, challenge authority. I took the photograph home and meditated on the meaning of this fierce quality and how I had developed it so early in life. I was disturbed and needed to understand why she came into my life.

I remembered the roles that children often assume to cope

with the mixed messages of parents struggling with alcoholism. I realized that as much as I loathed Little Miss Perfect in my current life, she had protected me as a child in emotionally confusing situations. She was a combination of attitudes and survival mechanisms that allowed me to negotiate a difficult home situation for many years, scrutinizing everything relentlessly to avoid the scenes so disturbing to a child's mind and heart. I felt I had come to the core of Little Miss Perfect's reason for being.

At that early phase of my life, Little Miss Perfect was not such a negative aspect. It isn't pretty that a six-year-old girl has to shield so much, but it's amazing and wonderful that my essence created that protective device. I thought, "Maybe Little Miss Perfect isn't so bad. Maybe she's just inappropriate — I've outgrown my need for her. Maybe I won't kill her off. Maybe I don't have to purge her. Instead of fighting with her for control, maybe I can make peace with her."

In a journal dialogue, I talked things over with her. I thanked her for what she had done for me. I reminded her (and in doing so, reminded myself) that I no longer live with alcoholics or other people from whom I need to protect myself. I don't need to be so rigid and controlling. I no longer need to know what's happening every minute, to speculate endlessly on what other people are thinking and feeling. I no longer need my "antennas" out at all times. My environment is no longer so unpredictably threatening.

Little Miss Perfect told me that she cared about me, she wanted my life to be peaceful and secure. She wanted to look out for me, to make sure I wouldn't get drawn into some argument or conflict I couldn't handle. She told me she didn't trust people, especially those who were close to me. We agreed that there were probably some appropriate places for her to use her skills in my life, and that we would work together to find them. I had cracked the code of Little Miss Perfect.

Since then, I have asked Little Miss Perfect to focus her attention on my business activities, particularly in seeking new markets, arranging my travel schedule, and negotiating my contracts — she's my business agent! She is enjoying this new station and is learning to love me in appropriate and helpful ways. I didn't have to kill her off. I would have lost a loyal friend and ally if I had.

When working with internal voices, particularly the ones representing negative messages, look for the "flip side," the positive opposites of the script. You may discover a hidden ally being drowned out by the louder, more persistent voice of the negative message.

The Little Miss Perfect journey is one that I share to illustrate that getting to know your voices may lead you into a phase of journalwork where you can crack the code of behavior that has you unconsciously locked into rigid, outdated decision-making patterns that hold you back from creative, self-loving energy.

In this way, your journal serves as a vital link to your self-direction. By increasing your self-knowledge, listening to internal voices and becoming familiar with patterns, you can take a more active part in developing behavior that supports a value system of your own choosing, rather than reacting to your past or reflecting old conditioning that may or may not represent your current beliefs and goals. As your self-awareness and consciousness evolve, you can make decisions based on who you are and what you want today, listening to the voices of self-knowledge and self-love. You can choose to let those voices set your priorities and direction, creating an inner environment of nurture, flexibility, and respect for growth.

Because our programmed voices intervene, like static on a telephone line, it is sometimes hard to tune in clearly to our actual feelings in the present moment. To bypass the voices of conditioning, and to hear the essential voice of the present, try using the following exercise.

Exercise: *Check-In*

Practice this tool for listening to your essential self. Finish these sentences, focusing only on the present moment.

I feel _____

I need _____

I want _____

The first sentence, "I feel _____," is simply a report on your emotion of the moment. Angry, frustrated, happy, bored, tense, irritated, excited, joyful—feelings are like weather, always changing. The Check-in is a weather report, outdated as soon as it's completed.

The second one, "I need _____," is usually a statement about nurturing, something that will support and facilitate your growth. You might need food, a nap, advice, solitude, attention, affection.

The third one, "I want _____," will state your desire, often about how you would prefer that your need be fulfilled. "I want my sweetheart to come over for dinner and listen to my problems with my manuscript." You may find out that your sweetheart has other plans, or has already eaten, or is preoccupied with her or his own problems. Then you'll have to figure out another way to fulfill your need. But you'll know what your preference is!

Most people find the Check-in to be surprisingly difficult, but it isn't really so surprising. When we acknowledge our feelings, and admit what our needs and wants are, it is almost impossible to ignore them. The Check-in is invaluable for helping you stay in touch with your most immediate self, and taking that self into consideration when you make decisions. After all, if you can't finish the Check-in sentences, on what information are you basing your decisions?

Now that we have uncovered the voice of our essential self, we find some new friends waiting patiently for us in the realm of the spirit.

INNER VIEW

If you could trade places with anyone, living or dead, who would it be and why?

INNER VIEW

How would your best friend describe you?

Spirit: Accessing Intuition

5

WHEN WE SHARE FROM the intuitive level in our intimacies, we experience an ineffable sense of connection with one another. Sometimes the feeling is immediate and positive. We might say, "Though we've just met, I feel as if I've known you for years!" Or, with no logical explanation, we have a compelling suspicion about someone right away. In our long-term intimacies, we might describe our connection as "psychic" when we get a telephone call from a friend just after having thought of them, or when letters written at the same time cross in the mail.

Intuition bypasses rationalization and linear thought, producing instead a resonance with the heart on a purely feeling level. It draws from the innate wisdom we bring into the world at birth, and although most of us experience intuition as unpredictable "flashes," it is as natural to us as our other five senses. Because society does not value intuitive abilities, we reach adulthood with precious little awareness of them—and what we do perceive, we discount.

Intuition is valuable precisely *because* it bypasses the rational mind. In addition, it bypasses conditioning and prejudice as well, communicating through insight—the direct apprehension of the inner nature. In other words, intuition is a direct *connection* with the inner nature. We might say we are communicating with and from the soul, spirit, or psyche. As we grow more intimate with our selves, we discover that when we access it, the intuition is a source of personal power. Fortunately, accessing intuition is a skill like any other. The more we use it, the stronger it becomes.

Images, symbols, meditation, play, and other nonlinear approaches sidestep the sentry of the rational mind and enable us to follow the subtle and often elusive path to the subconscious, where our intuitive aspects reside. Like friends who have been neglected for a long time, these aspects may be reticent to emerge at first. Try this simple exercise to open the door to your intuition.

Exercise: *Imagetrip*

Find an image that interests you, a postcard or magazine picture. You don't have to know why, just find an image that attracts your attention. Put it in plain view and make a journal entry by free-associating as you look at the image. Write anything that comes to your mind—it doesn't have to make sense, just let it flow. While you may encounter difficulty at first, you will be delighted at the fascinating connections you make, as you bypass your rational process and draw on your intuition.

Dreams, oracles, and shrines are three tools we can use in conjunction with journalwork for accessing and developing intuition. Each of them calls forth different aspects of our spiritual nature I have given names: dreams evoke the Fool, oracles the Elder, and shrines the Elf. While our scripted internal voices represent specific parts of our societal conditioning, these intuitive voices emerge from and articulate the deeper realms of our essential selves.

The Fool is that aspect of ourselves that is open to magic. The Fool in us takes risks, is full of awe and curiosity, and relates to the world with wonder and trust—childlike innocence is the Fool's trademark. Well-known as the beginning card of the tarot, and as the Clown in Native American symbolism, the Fool is usually the wisest member of the community, fully present in the moment and ready for whatever comes next. It is in our dreams we become the Fool, for in our dreams we are the guests of our intuition. Anything can happen and does: we can walk through walls, fly, swim underwater for hours, talk to animals, and communicate with the dead. We accept these abilities without question, moving through the dream, ready for magic. Every night, our rational minds take a holiday as we enter the world of dreams.

The Elder is that aspect of ourselves that sees the connection among all things, and speaks from that broad perspective. The Elder represents ancient wisdom, passed from one generation to the next through ritual and symbol. It is the Elder in us who offers guidance, advice, and comfort based on a deep trust in the intrinsic goodness of the universe. The Elder speaks through oracles, such as tarot cards, the I Ching, and the rune stones, all ancient symbol systems common to nearly every culture in the world.

The Elf is that aspect of ourselves that is always ready to play. When we open to the Elf in us, we are able to celebrate the ordinary and experience it in an extraordinary way. The Elf might enjoy hiding treasures for us to find on a walk around the neighborhood or directing our attention to synchronicities that bode good fortune—a flight of geese in formation against a magnificent sunset or a penny in our path. We beckon the Elf through creating shrines, special spaces especially made to reflect and celebrate the intuitive in our daily surroundings.

When we learn to call upon the inner Fool, Elder, and Elf for support and guidance, we are learning to trust our essential selves. This trust is at the heart of self-intimacy. Using the tools of dreams, oracles, and shrines in journalkeeping strengthens our communication with these powerful internal friends. By documenting intuitive experiences, journalwork reflects the unseen world of our psychic, spiritual selves.

Dreams: Evoking the Fool

In dreams, we can observe the mind at play. Dream images come from an intuitive source unharnessed by rationality. The activity in dreams is often bizarre, disregarding completely what is possible in "reality." The information we can gather about ourselves in dreams is unique in that it is not filtered through conscious, logical processes—it is wild, direct from the subconscious, and unavailable anywhere else. Not even our most conscientious journalkeeping of our waking life will render the clues we can discover about ourselves in our dreams.

The Fool, that part of us who participates actively in dreams, ventures beyond consciousness into other realms of psychic awareness. By becoming more attentive to our dream life, we experience ourselves as willing to risk unpredictable situations, to welcome unexpected changes, and to accept the abundant treasures of the psyche. When we bring the Fool to consciousness, we add a magical dimension to our "coping" ability allowing us to look beyond the obvious and find creative directions.

Recording dreams as a part of regular journal entries weaves them into the chronology of conscious life, placing them in a context. Often, their relationship to waking activities and concerns will reveal their meaning. In context, a dream often takes on significance beyond its surface content.

Sometimes dreams function as a setting where issues I am unready to deal with on a conscious level introduce themselves, a kind of surfacing point. Other times, dreams serve as a workspace for inner struggles about which I am in conscious denial.

An example concerns a series of dreams I had several years ago about a dental problem. When doing some unrelated journal study, I noticed several dreams about my teeth falling out and that the dreams were becoming more frequent and more vivid. Discovering those dreams was a surprise to me. On a deep level, I knew I needed to go to the dentist, (at the time I hadn't been in ten years), but I was avoiding it, cramming my concern into my subconscious. Only in reviewing the journal entries of dreams did I confront my inner concern for my dental health and make the necessary steps to care for myself. My rational mind was blocking the intuitive desire for wellness, but that nurturing energy found a way to get my attention.

Finally, dreams can function as an intuitive conversation with the self. Over time, I observe similar dream settings, and recognize familiar characters and symbols. I have experimented with requesting dreams and programming certain issues or questions into my dreams. "Lucid dreaming," or developing a conscious awareness within a dream, is especially exciting. Including dreams in your journal easily and naturally affirms your psychic dimension, adding depth to your self-intimacy.

REMEMBERING DREAMS

Some people say they never dream. Although everyone dreams, some of us remember our dreams, while others do not. With simple preparation and intention, you can dramatically enhance your dream recall by following these suggestions.

1. *Affirm your desire to remember your dreams.* As you prepare for sleep, acknowledge that you want to remember your dreams. This suggestion serves as an assurance to your inner self that you are interested in and committed to becoming aware of your dreams. As you say "yes" to remembering dreams, clear your mind of the day's activities and concerns. This act paves the way for dreams to appear.

2. *Keep your journal by your bed.* Open it to the appropriate page, date it, and write "Dream #1." This is another affirmation of your desire, and makes it easy for you to record your dream. If you must go to another room to

search for your journal in the middle of the night, you can bet you will not capture your dream.

3. *Tell your sleepmate what you are doing.* If you have a sleepmate, explain that you are attempting to catch your dreams. That way, if awakened by your feverish scribbling, your mate will understand and won't interrupt the fragile recording process.

4. *Keep a flashlight or penlight handy so you can avoid turning on the light.* A regular lamp can disturb others and scatter dream energy with brightness. A lower light will allow the dream to remain vivid as you enter consciousness.

5. *Record your dream as soon as you are aware of it.* During the night, you may awaken in the midst of a strong, vivid dream. It will seem so clear, you'll hear a voice saying, "I'll remember this in the morning. I'll wait and write it down then." Be warned: this voice is lying! While you may recall a few scraps of the dream, the scope of detail you garner when you record the dream immediately is astonishing, and well worth the effort.

6. *Write whatever you remember.* Upon awakening, ask yourself if you dreamed. Write anything you recall—fragments, words, images. Writing down partial images serves as another gesture of interest to your internal self and often stimulates further recall.

7. *Write in present tense.* Instead of saying, "I saw a green horse running towards me," say, "I see a green horse running towards me." This simple shift in tense will return you to the dream and you will experience it again in a direct way. You are in the dream, not detached from it. When I began using this suggestion, my ability to recall dream details increased dramatically.

If you keep a separate journal just for dreams, make a short entry in your daily journal to put each dream in its appropriate chronological place. Describe the dream in a few lines so when studying your journal later on, you will be able to observe its proximity to other events in your life. If you notice a connection, you can refer to your dream journal for the complete description.

Our essential selves communicate with us in dreams, using a highly symbolic language to express the concerns of our psyche and spirit. When we begin to pay attention to our dreams, recording and interpreting them, we are bridging the gap between our rational and intuitive realms. The sharing of dreams marks a tender time in the evolution of intimacy, a time when rigid boundaries between what is considered "real" and "unreal" relax in a safe and sacred space of trust.

Exercise: *Dream Catching*

Tonight, open the workbook to this page and place it by your bed. Make sure you have a pen or pencil next to it, and write the date and "Dream #1." Affirm your desire to remember your dreams, and trust that you will. Sweet dreams!

Oracles: Evoking the Elder

In ancient times, people who wished to communicate with the "divine" often consulted the oracles, usually with the guidance of a priestess. Oracles could be a scattering of etched stones, the reading of clouds or animal movements, or the tossing of yarrow sticks. The symbols represented the cycles of nature, the structure of society and community, the journey of the soul through its many evolutions and incarnations, and the same fascinating link with the collective unconscious held in our dream images. Found in almost every culture, oracles have been passed from one generation to the next over thousands of years and offer what I call the wisdom of the internal Elder. Today, some common oracles are the tarot cards, I Ching coins and the rune stones, each of which I will describe in this chapter.

When asked, the Elder gives advice and wise counsel in times of frustration and impatience. I use oracles as a way to still my surface chatter and to shift from the tunnel vision of daily activities to a broader perspective. Oracles are a form of meditation and spiritual play. The magical, prophetic power claimed by the ancient oracle-users is real; I have a profound respect for the oracles' ability to illuminate hidden aspects of my life. At the same time, I am clear that the wisdom I discover is my own. In other words, I've never learned something from an oracle I didn't already know.

The oracles serve as gentle guides to help me reach levels of knowledge I have not yet brought to consciousness. Symbolized as the Elder, oracles provide a setting in which I can safely release rational control and open myself to a broader range of possibilities. They are wonderful devices of pleasure, adventure, comfort, and hope. I have found them to be delightful companions and mirrors of my growing personal power.

I call on the Elder for a variety of reasons, and you will find different circumstances for seeking the assistance of oracles. Here are some possibilities.

1. *To break the "set" of your mind and attitude when you are attached to or stuck in a certain way of thinking; when you are immersed so deeply in the logical, you cannot entertain another perspective.*

2. *To break a lengthy silence in your journal.*
3. *To challenge a stubborn confusion or ambivalence.*
4. *To mark special passages, such as birthdays, anniversaries, or holidays.*
5. *To probe deeper into dreams or memories.*
6. *To achieve new insights into old problems.*
7. *To encourage your mind to use images instead of words.*
8. *To allow your mind to relax and* play!

In the simplest sense, oracles provide an easy way to make a journal entry when you don't feel like writing. The sequence of using oracles requires that you focus your attention and pose a question. This in itself helps describe where you are with yourself at that moment. Whether or not you choose to react to your consultation, the entry of the date, the question, and the oracle's response alone will give ample information concerning your current situation. And the potential for the oracle exercise to stimulate more insightful writing is very high.

HOW TO USE AN ORACLE

The way to consult an oracle is the same whether using the tarot, I Ching or runes. The simple four-step ritual that follows quietens the surface voices, focuses attention on deeper levels of awareness, and evokes the wisdom of the inner Elder.

1. *Acknowledge your desire to use an oracle.* This step tells you that you are at a particular juncture with your self-observation, or that you are at a point in your creative cycle when you want additional information, assistance, or outside opinions. The desire to use an oracle is in itself a clue to the current situation.

2. *Pose a question.* This step presses you to identify specifically the issue, feeling, relationship or situation that concerns you. Once you have admitted your concern with an issue by posing a question for the oracle, you have already gained some knowledge about what is going on at a deeper level. While general or open-ended questions such as "What's happening in my life?" can sometimes be helpful, the more specific your question,

the more revealing the answer will be. This is because in challenging yourself to name your true concerns, you are able to recognize the cause of many problems. However, you will discover that regardless of your question, the oracles will address your actual concern, whether or not you have accurately named it.

3. *Surrender to the random order.* Once the question is posed, each oracle requires that the querent (the one asking the question) relinquish control of the oracle and invest it with power. This is done by shuffling the cards, tossing the coins, or shaking up the bag of rune stones. There is a feeling of relief: "I'll let the cards figure this one out!" In fact, this turning over of power is a surrendering to the deep inner wisdom you hold at your core. The oracle silences the superficial chatter and preconceived notions obscuring the wisdom of the Elder from your conscious mind.

4. *Thoughtfully consider the oracle's response.* Once the oracles have been laid out, observe the information and respond to the images you have chosen. Meditate on the ancient symbols, and take note of the images, feelings, and ideas that are evoked in you.

By following the sequence, you clear your mind, focus it, and listen: the process helps to clarify your awareness. I have realized that even if the oracles depicted nonsense images such as cars, frogs, and apples rather than ancient mystical archetypes, I would probably gain a new perspective on my question by following the sequence of clearing, focusing, and listening. Rather than viewing this as a trivialization of the oracles' power, I see it as an affirmation of my own power to gain insight through trusting and attending to my inner wisdom.

The journal entries provoked by oracle work are delightfully revealing in several ways. They hold the clues of the question and timing; that is, when I choose to consult an oracle and which one. Scanning past journals, I notice I often ask about the same issues, or I go through a phase of asking the oracles about everything. My response to specific castings never fails to give me greater insight, and when I review these sessions after the situation in question is resolved, I can check the "accuracy" of the oracles' advice, and my interpretations.

When using oracles in journalwork, date your entry, record your question, and record the answer of the oracle. After meditating on the images, write a short summary of your reaction. You may spend five minutes, or five hours, but the essential information is contained in your simple question and answer.

The world of oracles is rich, vast, and ancient. Many fine books are available that cover the origin and use of the oracles through the ages; I have listed some of my favorites in the Resources section at the end of the workbook, and several of them are designed as workbooks for beginners. If you are completely unfamiliar with oracles, here is a brief description of the tarot cards, the I Ching coins, and the rune stones. You can usually find them at bookstores specializing in metaphysics, women, or "new age" information.

The tarot cards: This deck has seventy-eight cards representing an ancient Western occult psychological and philosophical system. In archetypal symbols, the Tarot depicts the journey of the soul's evolution, and how that journey is acted out in an individual lifetime. Our contemporary playing cards are derived from the tarot. A reading is done by shuffling the deck, selecting the cards randomly, and arranging them in a pattern or "spread" in which each card has a specific meaning. The result is a symbolic picture revealing the current influence relating to your question.

I Ching: Also known as the *Book of Changes,* I Ching is attributed by some to Ken Wen who lived between 1150–249 B.C. in China. This body of wisdom draws upon the cycles of nature, the formation and disintegration of social structures, and the constant evolution and change of life. The symbol system consists of sixty-four hexagrams, six-lined patterns that are obtained most often by the tossing of three coins or many yarrow sticks. The combination of heads and tails forms the hexagram; there are sixty-four possible configurations. Each hexagram corresponds to messages about balance, change and power. Filled with poetic imagery of nature, I Ching offers an

Eastern perspective on the intuitive source. When consulting I Ching, you are said to be consulting the Sage, the wise one.

The runes: These smooth, flat stones with glyphs or symbols carved on one side, possibly originated in ancient Scandinavia or Germany. In their contemporary form, the runic alphabet consists of twenty-four symbols. Their messages trace the path of the Spiritual Warrior, whose quest is self-development and inner transformation. The stones are usually carried in a bag, and are shaken and tossed to select the appropriate ones for a reading. They can be arranged in spreads similar to the tarot cards for specific castings.

Shrines: Evoking the Elf

A shrine is a sanctuary, a place where we honor those things we hold sacred and precious. Most of us are familiar with shrines only in the context of our religious practices yet in all probability, we have made and used shrines throughout our lives. If you look around your home, you are likely to find a group of family photographs carefully arranged on the mantle or bookshelf. Perhaps you notice a diploma framed on the wall, or trophies and ribbons from winning competitions. There might be a display of your collections, such as butterflies, stamps, or bells. Often souvenirs from your travels will find a special place of display. The Elf in us gathers these objects together and sets them apart to draw attention to them and to honor their place in our lives.

When we bring this practice to a conscious level, we create a shrine: an intentional arranging of objects to invest them with meaning, to draw attention to them for symbolic purposes, or to honor a feeling or accomplishment. Shrines are a special extension of journalkeeping which allows intuition, or our inner Elf, to make associations and connections without asking for a logical reason. As you watch a shine develop over time, new dimensions of your essential self will unfold before your eyes.

My introduction to shrines as a tool for self-observation came from Janie, a visual artist, friend, and former neighbor. Whenever I visited Janie, I was struck by the visual richness of her living space. She would tack anything to the wall: feathers, bones, scraps of bright ribbon, postcards, rough sketches of future drawings. She explained that she liked to "feed" herself visually by surrounding herself with colors and textures that would inspire her artwork. I christened her apartment "The Magic Museum," for it had an enchanting effect on me, and I always left feeling refreshed, excited, and creatively stimulated. Janie's Elf was free to decorate, celebrate, and delight the senses. Upon returning to my home, I would notice the stacks of musty magazines, newspapers, and books. The walls were bare, my closets full of rolled posters awaiting frames. Evidence of my Elf was nowhere to be seen. I decided to try feeding myself visually as Janie suggested. Slowly and timidly, putting up the posters with tape and tacks, I began coaxing out my Elf. On my nightstand, I placed a shell next to a candle. I ventured to buy a few cut flowers, and I was on my way.

What I discovered as I stretched my sensory antennae, was that my environment is both an influence on my internal world and an expression of it. Whether or not I am intentional about constructing my environment, it affects me, for the objects surrounding me have meaning and convey information, subliminally at the very least. Can you find evidence of your Elf?

Exercise: *Shrine Watch*

Look around your home, noticing any group of objects that attract your attention or that you encounter on a daily basis. Ask yourself what each group "says" to you or about you. (A pile of dirty laundry might be a comment about being overworked on the job, a refrigerator covered with snapshots a statement of your wide circle of friends.) Observe which of these shrines you made consciously, and which unconsciously. Are there some shrines you deliberately avoid? Others you gravitate towards? Record your experience, describing some of the shrines and their meanings.

Shrines reflect inner concerns and invoke intuition, inviting it to come out and play. As a tool for exploring the interior world, shrines are part of journalkeeping: shrines are three-dimensional journal entries, just as real as the most fluent prose.

To make a shrine, start with a space you will encounter daily so that it will attract attention. Good shrine spots are mantles, window sills, bedside tables, bookshelves, or the top of the television. Then decide whether the shrine will be exploratory or have a conscious theme.

If it is exploratory, begin with an object that attracts your attention simply because of its beauty, uniqueness, or peculiarity. No reason is necessary. Perhaps someone has given you a lovely crystal, or you have a funny souvenir from a recent trip. Put this object in a shrine spot and allow your Elf to add other items to it as you feel the impulse, without asking why or searching for a rational connection. Shrines don't need a "why." I have found that an exploratory shrine might grow for months—I will shift its position, add more objects, rearrange them, without an inkling of what the shrine symbolizes. Eventually, and somewhat suddenly, the shrine will "ripen." All the necessary objects are present, I just know it. Then, one day as I am staring at these favorite things, the significance of the shrine will emerge like a psychic telegram. It may be a clear feeling, a new goal revealing itself, or a secret I've been keeping from myself. Often, shrines symbolize my deeper spiritual concerns and provide a safe space for me to encounter them.

Making a shrine with a theme can help clarify specific issues, too. Select an object that reminds you of the situation in question—maybe you're struggling with a relationship conflict, or you want to remember your dreams. Place the object in a designated shrine spot. Soon, that object will attract another, a postcard or photograph, a special rock, or a bright piece of fabric. Your Elf will look for things to add to the arrangement, and on a subliminal level the shrine will remind you in a gentle and playful manner of the issue at hand. Your attention, consciously and unconsciously, will be focused on the theme and you will be alert to clues that will deepen your understanding of it.

Often, the need for a shrine will become apparent to you from the kinds of entries you're making in your journal—repetitive, whiney, stuck in a bog, obsession with a single issue, fear, dread, confusion. Creating a shrine gives you a way to address these feelings and take action without forcing confrontation. Like your journal, shrines provide a sacred space for your internal concerns. Shrines can be documented by photographing, drawing, or simply describing them in your journal, but the real power of shrines comes from making and watching them.

Exercise: *Beginning a Shrine*

Find an object that symbolizes your desire to develop self-intimacy through journalkeeping. Begin a shrine by placing the object in a special space you will encounter daily. Listen for your Elf, and watch the shrine grow.

The Fool, Elder, and Elf are just a few of the positive aspects we have within us. As you did in the previous chapter, you can give these parts of yourself names—such as Guide, Ally, Coach, Angel, Higher Self, Crone—in order to honor their presence in your life and to become more familiar with their influence.

INNER VIEW

Do you believe in universal principles, such as "killing is wrong"? Describe your personal version of universal principles.

Sharing Wisdom: 6
Pattern Detection

*M*Y OLDEST FRIENDSHIP is with June. We met as seniors in college and have maintained our intimacy for over eighteen years, through marriages, divorces, different cities, different jobs, and disagreements. What I value the most about the relationship is our ability to spot recurring habits in each other's lives. We are able to do this because we have shared the details of individual process through the years, we remember each other's history, and we trust and expect each other to tell the truth. Sharing the wisdom of our insights has not always been easy or comfortable, but our willingness to do so is evidence of our intimacy's depth.

As you cultivate a deep level of intimacy with yourself through journalkeeping, you are accumulating a history of sharing, remembering, and honesty. The volumes themselves represent time spent in tender attentiveness and become an encyclopedia of self. These precious resource books hold information that does not exist anywhere else in the universe. You can read them like a series of novels, or study them like textbooks. When you return to them as a reader, you find that individual choices have coalesced, revealing broad directions. By studying your journals, you begin to notice patterns, cycles, and habits of behavior—physical, mental, emotional, and spiritual. These patterns indicate the ways in which energy is being directed, consciously or unconsciously. By increasing awareness of repetitive behaviors and seeing them in the ongoing context of your life, you can assess which ones are helpful and which are outdated. Journalkeeping—the writing freely over time—leaves a trail of breadcrumbs through the forest which you can follow backwards to discover your path. You may find that you need to chart a new course, or that your navigational skills are surprisingly accurate. Before you can study your journals, however, you must read them.

Reading one of your journals feels like a visit from a dear friend who lives in a distant city. You listen to and give detailed accounts of the many episodes that make up a life, and late in the night, after many such stories are shared, you declare yourselves "caught up." Or, in an analogy to the therapeutic relationship, when you write in the journal, you are the client—talking freely and openly to a sympathetic ear. When you read the journal, you are the therapist—listening attentively, without judgement or criticism, but sensitive to the overall picture.

Some people who write conscientiously in their journals do not ever read them, finding them to be "too painful," "too embarrassing," or "totally boring!" The majority of these people primarily use journalkeeping for catharsis, to let off steam when angry or to express other strong emotions, generally negative ones. Much later, they discover this habit creates a distorted portrait of a life, much like the fun house at a carnival, full of crazy mirrors. One woman, after doing her workshop assignment of reading over past journals, remarked, "I think I've been depressed for three years!" Most likely her life was filled with the normal ups and downs that we all experience, but she had not recorded that rich variety. In reading over her journals, she discovered a pattern: her self-intimacy was focused solely around depression. Have you ever had a friend who called you only when upset, angry, in crisis, or depressed? Reading over your journals will reveal the character of your self-intimacy.

Another complaint about reading past journals is that "they all sound alike." You may feel you are writing the same things year after year, and get discouraged, thinking that you haven't made any progress. If you find that past journals sound just like your current one, take heart: repetition is the main clue to pattern detection, and when you identify your patterns, you can choose whether or not you want to follow them. This is precisely why reading the journals is so valuable, to spot unconscious obedience to old patterns. I know of no other process that documents these invisible habits where they can be observed.

Resistance to reading past journals may come from the tendency to self-criticize. When you look back at former entries, you are reading from the vantage point of the "future" with the benefit of hindsight. Understandably, your perception will be different now than at the time of your entry, so you must be generous to that prior self. You have the advantage of context. You know what happened next!

To avoid the pitfall of self-criticism when you begin to read a completed journal, suspend judgement and criticism. Give yourself the gentle compassion extended to a dear friend who has asked for a sounding board. Remember that you have encouraged yourself to write freely, without concern for a reader. While reading your entries, resist the temptation to impose a retroactive editor or critical parent. Instead, listen quietly as you read, taking note of interesting connections without judgement.

Remember also that in the context of an intimacy, the privilege of reading someone's journal is a rare and precious gift of vulnerability. Imagine your sweetheart or best friend asking you to read a volume, and extend the same sensitivity to yourself. You may learn things that are difficult to accept or understand, but the purpose of this deep sharing is to increase the quality of intimacy and honesty within you. Respect the courage it takes to risk this level of self-knowledge.

Reading your current journal increases self-awareness in a special way. Every month or six weeks, take time to "visit" yourself by reading over your recent entries. This will develop your sense of context and continuity, and encourage you to appreciate the complexity of your life. Whether our lives are simplified by routine, or disrupted by the unexpected, we all operate on many different levels of experience and awareness. Because we focus on one thing at a time, we tend to forget how many concerns we are juggling at once. You can get your bearings by reading your current journal, taking note of accomplishments you want to affirm or stressful situations that may be unattended. You may notice the beginnings of a pattern — several complaints about a co-worker, or a series of disturbing dreams — and choose to alter your behavior.

After accumulating volumes for a few years, try looking back at particular dates, such as your birthday, a holiday, or the anniversary of an event. Because these moments have special significance, they will often trigger more reflective entries, or at least more powerful memories. Reading back through them creates a long-range perspective in which you compare concerns of the present to concerns of the past, gaining a relative view of your progress using the arbitrary structure of the date. Using this technique, I discovered that for at least ten years, the month of May held unexpected and dramatic twists of fate for me: my apartment would be sold, a friend would move across the country, I would lose or get a job — always in May. This discovery helped me document a personal yearly growth cycle, correlated to the seasons as well as astrology.

"Hearing" a journal is different from simply reading it. While reading a journal reveals obvious patterns, hearing a journal is an intuitive awareness of the undercurrent patterns rarely stated directly. The sensation of hearing a journal is that of reading between the lines. Hearing takes place after gaining a certain distance and detachment from the self that wrote the entries. It comes from gaining the perspective that only time and distance can offer, after wounds have healed, tempers cooled, frustrations eased, lessons learned. Usually a year or more must pass from the time of writing. I can hear a journal when I have evolved past a prior self. In fact, hearing a past journal often feels as if I am reading the words of another person entirely.

For example, after my marriage ended in my early twenties, I read and reread the journals I had kept. I wanted so much to understand what had happened, yet the entries simply frustrated and depressed me. I was still in the midst of the identity search which had contributed to my decision to divorce. Finally, feeling that I had recorded nothing of value, I put the journals away. When I pulled them out recently to work on some class exercises, I was struck by a single line, set apart from a page filled with ordinary entries. In all capitals I had written, "SEWING MY OWN CLOTHES SEEMS VULGAR TO ME."

At first I laughed: how could sewing be *vulgar?* But suddenly I heard this bizarre remark, fifteen years later, as the powerful symbol that it was. I recalled how I hated sewing as an adolescent but was made to learn, how I sewed my own clothes in college to conserve money, and how I moved on to draperies and slipcovers as a wife. There in my journal, I heard the voice of my emerging self stating her opinion—extreme as it was—that sewing was now considered vulgar. That self was determined to find a way out of the stifling structure of marriage, symbolized at that moment by sewing. My laughter was filled with compassion for the unhappy young woman who burst out of a role that did not suit her.

It is worth noting that a sentence which at the moment of writing certainly seemed totally inconsequential, years later became the key to deeper intimacy and self-acceptance. This underscores the importance of writing freely, without judgement, allowing yourself to express anything, everything, and trusting that time will give you the wisdom to sort through your outpourings.

When can you expect to hear a journal? There seem to be two elements that grant the ability to hear a past journal. First, *time*. When enough time has passed, or enough changes lived through, the necessary distance will be gained. This will vary according to the events contained in the journal; in the example cited above, nearly fifteen years had to pass. In general, I find that after at least one year, and usually within three years, I notice the ability to hear.

The second element is *shock*. An unexpected turn in fortune's wheel can radically shift your consciousness, altering your perspective so completely that you feel like a different person. A decision to change careers, a move to another city, an illness or accident, the break-up or beginning of a relationship—in cases like this, you will be able to hear your current journal immediately, you will feel so detached from your "previous" life.

Studying journals is a form of self-examination that requires trust. While most journalwork is based on the suspension of judgement and analysis, detecting personal patterns by studying journals is accomplished by applying critical abilities, albeit in a tender and loving manner. If you cannot trust yourself to be kind, I suggest you allow your self-intimacy to deepen further before you study your journals.

My own discovery of this powerful aspect of journalkeeping was not intentional. I began to study my journals when I was writing a novel, in the process of combing through old journals for character sketches, settings, and plotlines. I was looking for ways to combine the qualities of several people into a single character, and to trace the development of certain issues to construct the narrative thread of my fictional story. I wanted to structure the novel like a journal, revealing the main character through her entries. I found myself reading through past journals with a highlighting marker, making charts, diagrams, and maps. A meticulous cross-referencing system evolved for a full year's worth of journals until one day, I began to feel strange. I had a sense of going too far, a feeling that I was breaking a taboo, reading after "lights out," or doing something expressly forbidden.

I walked out of my workroom into the sun on my porch and sat in the hammock. As I tuned into myself and considered my feelings, I heard a snide comment coming from an internal voice: "You write them, you read them, now you *study* them. What's next, the *movie?*" I was encountering a strong resistance to the deep introspection my research had prompted. It occurred to me that this resistance might indicate I was onto something important. I now believe that the cultural taboo against self-observation and self-loving—often described cynically as selfishness, self-absorption, or self-centeredness— inhibits us from exploring our individual spiritual paths, lest we rattle society's cage with our creativity and distinction.

My experience with self-examination is that each of us holds special wisdom available when we have the courage to look at ourselves in relation to the world. Inadvertently, when I began to study my journals and to honor them as precious resource books, I broke through to a new level of understanding and appreciation for myself. I felt an awareness of my contribution and potential, and an excitement as I saw my destiny unfolding through the struggles and celebrations recorded in my journal.

The following two techniques, *scanning* and *scrutiny*, describe ways to work with past journals.

Scanning

Scanning is a process of quickly reviewing a journal volume to extract specific clues that will reveal possible patterns in actions, thoughts, feelings, and choices. The sensation of scanning is like reviewing for an exam: reading quickly through a block of information looking for the most important facts, or ideas that will help trigger memory and connect the information. Scanning creates a context, allowing you to see the continuum of movement rather than isolated, random memories. As if watching a film, you condense time into a narrative and experience the sequential chronology of your life. This overview perspective will begin to reveal the cycles, the ebb and flow of changes represented in your journal.

Recalling the metaphor of the archaeology dig in Chapter Three, on memory, scanning takes place back in the laboratory, after the fieldwork is done and the samples of potential artifacts are gathered in the lab. The archaeologist must survey the entire cache before analyzing any one item. In scanning, you begin to shift into a more objective perspective, looking for possible connections that will deepen your self-understanding.

A scan can be intentional or random; that is, you may have a clear and specific focus of what you are looking for, or you may be looking at a certain period of time without a preconceived notion of what the issues were. A *focused* scan looks for specific information—about a person, a conflict, a relationship, dreams—or you may be interested in exploring how a particular incident (a health matter, the breakup of a relationship, or a sudden relocation) affected the overall patterns of your life. A *random* scan is open-ended: by allowing your intuitive eye/ear to pick up on subtle clues, your scan will reveal formerly invisible undercurrents throughout your daily choices. Either way, you will discover hidden information all through your journal.

Prepare to scan as you would for a Memory Probe. *Set up the environment* by making sure you have adequate safety and uninterrupted time, probably about two hours, according to how much material you are scanning. Then, *suspend analysis* — for although you will be looking for specific information and consequently making judgements to select what is pertinent and what is not, this is not the time to analyze or criticize. Check your negative self-talk or you may get bogged down in a quagmire of "How could I have been so stupid?" as you review the past. Next, *invite your internal editor to come along,* but be specific about the goal of your session. Clearly state what the purpose of the session is; for example, "I am gathering information about my relationship with my brother. I will analyze the information at a later time." This way, you can get the benefit of your critical abilities for selection purposes, without debilitating judgmental comments.

HOW TO SCAN

1. *Select a volume or volumes covering a six- to twelve-month period.*

2. *Decide whether this is a random or focused scan; in the case of a focused scan, specify the goal.*

3. *Read the entire time period in one sitting, without interruption, if possible.* This collapses the period covered in the volumes, creating in your mind a narrative continuum that you view as a whole. Often, it is tempting to dwell on a certain entry, getting lost in a particular moment, but this will distort the perspective Scanning is designed to create. When lingering occurs, make a date to come back to this entry at another time, and continue moving through your scan.

4. *Use a highlighter or brightly colored pen to mark significant phrases or sections.* Make a notation in the front of the journal indicating the date of the scan and the color used; you may return at another time for a different purpose and this notation will help you identify previous research. Moving quickly through the volume,

allow yourself to mark anything that attracts your attention.

5. *Review marks after completing the scan, making notes of any particular connections and impressions gathered.* Record what you feel, and ground yourself before moving on to another activity.

WHAT TO LOOK FOR WHILE SCANNING

○ *Repetition of any kind.* The repeated appearance of a person, issue, color, statement, dream, anything. Patterns are made up of repetition. Pick up on the exact elements of the sequence and the intervals between them. Observe the relationship of the repeated element to its context.

○ *Extremes.* Broad ranges of mood or attitude— depression, exhilaration, energy bursts, fatigue, worry, fear, tantrums, boredom, celebration, happiness, confidence.

○ *Anger.* Indicates the violation of a boundary or the taking of a stand. This is a form of personal definition. Examine the anger in the context of your life's narrative to discover dramatic patterns of energy: what was the object of the anger? Was it appropriately expressed and directed? Was it a cover for something deeper? What triggered the anger? How does the anger define your limits, boundaries, and self-definition?

○ *Inner voices.* New internal voices are often discovered or named during scanning. The roles they play and their "scripts" become much more obvious as you observe their relationship to other aspects of yourself.

○ *Silences.* The context surrounding the silences gives information on what prompted the silence, how long it lasted, and what motivated you to resume writing. By leaving a blank space for silences as recommended earlier, you will make it much easier to spot them while scanning.

○ *Ultimatums.* A specific kind of extreme expressing a definition point, a challenge, or covenant with the self; for example, "I'll never speak to her again," "From now on, I'll jog every day," "I'll write in my journal every day on my vacation," or "If he ever talks to me like that again, I'll leave him!" Sometimes, an ultimatum is triggered by an unconscious reaction to a restrictive pattern.

○ *Shifts in handwriting.* Handwriting is a barometer of mood. Observing shifts in handwriting during a scan increases self-intimacy on a subtle, subconscious level and develops familiarity with internal cycles that may otherwise be imperceptible.

○ *Dreams.* As with silences, dreams (especially recurring ones) can be revealing when observed in context.

○ *Amnesia.* Notice entries that seem to indicate you have forgotten recent incidents. This can be a clue to a cycle of denial.

This list is meant to provide a starting point for the gathering of clues. You will find many more, for scanning is a combination of intuition and conscious intention, a gathering of evidence, and a personal scavenger hunt. Once you have scanned, you will have a cluster of clues and perhaps a few pieces of a suspicious cycle or two.

If you have some completed journals, try the following exercise.

Exercise: *Scanning*

After scanning a volume, meditate for a few moments on
what you have experienced. Write a brief summary of
your feelings and immediate reactions. If you have
perceived major issues or trends, state them simply.

Now you are ready to scrutinize.

Scrutiny

I have a few deeply trusted friends whom I call upon for scrutiny. Because scrutiny is a request for evaluation, opinion, assessment, and analysis, I choose the source carefully when I need this kind of assistance from a friend. Hearing criticism, even loving and constructive criticism, is not one of my favorite pastimes. At the same time, I need clarity of vision, honesty, and the courage to tell the truth, even when it might hurt a little—or more than a little. Usually I want a friend who not only loves me, knows my history, and is a good listener, but also one who understands the tender firmness with which such advice must be given in order for it to be heard. To scrutinize myself, I must evoke these same qualities. Successful scrutiny is a testimony to the depth of intimacy and trust, whether with a friend or with yourself.

The goal of scrutiny is *insight*. The archaeologist studies each individual artifact, considering its possible connection to the many others, keeping in mind historical knowledge, current conditions, and speculations—all without ruling out the possibility of discovery as the entire panorama is surveyed. In scrutiny, rational and intuitive abilities are balanced, working in harmony to evaluate while remaining open to insight.

Because scrutiny employs critical thinking, there is the by now familiar danger of using it as an opportunity to beat yourself up, to needlessly berate yourself, to judge by unrealistic standards with the righteousness of 20/20 hindsight. If you find yourself falling prey to this tendency, stop and imagine going to a friend for scrutiny who, after listening to your open, honest and vulnerable disclosures, treats you abusively, listing your shortcomings, pointing out all your faults, and giving a lengthy description of all the other times you've erred in just this way. This friend would not be one you would confide in again.

In our intimacy with self, we have the opportunity to treat ourselves with the gentleness we long for. Replace your insensitive friend with one of your positive aspects, your angel, guide, elder, or crone who speaks with loving but detached interest in your continuing growth and happiness. From this perspective, you can acknowledge helpful insights in ways that are healing rather than destructive to your self-esteem.

HOW TO SCRUTINIZE
To begin, select a volume you have scanned, set up your environment, call in a positive aspect to accompany you, and then follow these steps.

1. *Review your scanning summary.* Decide what major aspects of the volume will be the object of your scrutiny exercise; for example, "discomfort with Pat's friendship," "desire for job change," "recurring dreams about brother."

2. *Extract pertinent information highlighted by scanning.* On a new journal page or a larger newsprint tablet, list out the "pieces of the puzzle" you feel are relevant. This may take the form of a chronology of events or it may be a selection of random facts you intuitively feel are related.

3. *Analyze.* This step can take many forms. In essence, you are examining the *parts* in relation to the *whole.* Having made the list in step two, you could categorize them into areas, then combine them in different ways to explore their relationships. For example, your scan may indicate that you are quietly obsessing about a job change. Your list could include a group of complaints about your present situation, fears about changing, qualities of your next position, and goals for the long-term, all culled from your journal by scanning. By dividing these into categories, you might discover a strategy for researching a new job direction that doesn't disrupt your current situation or income, while infusing some dynamic new energy into your routine. Or, after assessing your lists, you might decide that your goals for the long-term are best served by staying where you are — and that you must address your chronic complaints with a less dramatic alternative.
   Other analysis tools are diagrams, charts, or draw-

ings. These visual models of your experiences help break up preconceived notions and encourage experimentation. My scrutiny sessions often feel like I am "rearranging reality."

Partnership is an area often chosen for scrutiny. After studying your journals, you might find you've been having the same relationship for years, but with a series of different people; that is, your pattern of intimacy follows a similar cycle no matter who you are with. In such a case, your scrutiny analysis might define your intimacy cycle so clearly that you will be able to identify it in the early stages. By such self-awareness, you can choose to step outside of your habits, and tune in to the vital unpredictability of the present, thus creating the opportunity to have an authentic relationship with your current partner. Sometimes "old baggage" can get extremely heavy.

Scrutiny is where healing takes place: you are diagnosing what the problem is and assessing what changes are necessary to align yourself with your current goals. As you scrutinize, expect to feel a sensation of "Aha!" as insights resonate with inner wisdom. Suddenly, many parts of your experience will glow with this new knowledge and you will feel a sense of clarity. At this point, you may want to review other journals to test the perspective you've gained.

Sometimes, scrutiny will help identify areas you'd like additional help with, through counseling, therapy, or guidance from an astrologer, nutritionist, chiropractor, psychologist, or other healer. You'll find your journalwork has prepared you well, and that you bring to your sessions a grounded and purposeful self-awareness.

Through reading, scanning, and scrutiny, we experience a level of maturity in our self-intimacy that is deeply empowering. These aspects of journalkeeping give us a way to incorporate and appreciate change, rather than resist it, and in doing so, we can move with confidence into the future.

INNER VIEW

List your vices and virtues. Which are easier to name?

INNER VIEW

Do you have any regrets? What are they? Choose one and imagine you made a different choice. How would your present life be changed by your decision?

Personal Maps: Sharing the Future

S HARING PLANS FOR THE future marks a new dimension of closeness for any intimate relationship. Good friends become business partners; lovers become co-parents; neighbors decide to cultivate a garden. When we share our dreams and efforts, we draw on every aspect of intimacy— confessing fears, relating histories, understanding patterns, listening to our deepest voices, celebrating spirit. This transition demonstrates trust, confidence, and respect, not to mention a willingness to risk both failure and success. The intimacy that is engendered by working together draws us out of ourselves and into community so that our habits, styles, and personal idiosyncracies all become part of the creative process, right out in the open. In a group or partnership, one person's flagging confidence can be bolstered by the soaring hopes of another, and the conscientious effort required to achieve the goal at hand is shared by all. Without the benefit of a community's energy, sharing the future with yourself offers a different sort of challenge.

Over the years, I noticed that I was always eager to give over my energy to group efforts, whether in a business setting, a community or artistic project, or a political cause. I was a wonderful team player and liked nothing more than to work with people I loved on something in which I believed. Through my self-study, however, I found that as much satisfaction as I felt in these projects, I harbored a secret knowledge that I had abandoned myself. Would my journal book ever be written? Would I ever visit Bryce Canyon, Utah? Would I ever present my workshops in other cities? Would I ever learn tai chi? These were personal goals that, at least initially, required only my own effort. Yet I was forever putting them off, feeling the group project was more important. My secret knowledge of self-abandonment burrowed deeper, becoming a cold stone of resentment at the base of my tendency to feel—and act—like a martyr. Once I named this truth, I knew I had to pull away from groups for a while. I wanted to learn how to harness my energy toward my own personal goals, and to apply my knowledge about planning, goal-setting, and strategy to my dreams. I was ready to deepen my self-intimacy, and my journal was waiting for me, eager to help.

Until this point, most of the journalwork I've suggested has focused on the past or the present: searching memories for long-forgotten decisions, observing daily activity to discern rigid patterns, or listening more deeply to the essential self. But the journal can also be a tool for divining the future—or rather, *designing* the future. Just as we can become more conscious of aspects from our past and present that influence our behavior, we can become more aware of our desires in ways that allow us to actively participate in the construction of the future. Two terms from the world of aerial navigation describe specific areas of journalwork that foster healthy, positive, and conscious growth: *aiming,* which asks "What do I want?", and *attitude,* which asks "How do I get it?"

When an airplane takes off from its origination point, it is aimed carefully and precisely in the direction of its destination. In order for the plane to reach that location, the aim must be maintained constantly, regardless of what happens in flight. If the aim of the plane wavers, even for a moment, the plane gets off course. At the same time, the attitude of the plane is constantly changing. In navigational terms, a plane in motion has an attitude which determines where, how, and when it lands. The attitude is made up of the subtle tilt and pitch of the plane and must respond instantly to the myriad changes happening in flight: the wind picks up or shifts direction, the visibility alters, the weight of the plane lightens as the fuel is used. The combination of the constant aim and the fluid attitude allow the plane to reach its destination. This dynamic coalition is replicated in your own successful plan for reaching a destination of your own.

Aiming

The old saying, "If you don't know where you're going, any path will take you there," illustrates the importance of aiming. In order to focus your energy effectively, you must have at least an idea of where you want to go. Aiming asks, "What do I want?" It is a form of naming, a technique introduced with internal voices. With voices, the name describes something that already exists. With aiming, you name something *into* existence. Your destination is only another spot on the map until you choose it.

To help answer that exacting question, "What do I want?," practice journal activities that encourage open-ended, no-fault, no-goal entries: fantasizing, wishing, daydreaming, complaining, whining, hoping, meditating, playing, drawing, doodling. Oracles, shrines, and dreamwork are wonderful tools for strengthening the ability to tune in to the little kid inside who is still in touch with desire. Allow yourself to *play* in your journal. This connection to the inner child will come in handy when circumstances force you to identify your want—what you *really* want, not what society, family, or the internal "shoulds" insist that you want. But don't wait for a crisis situation to check in with your desires. If you do, you may find it impossible to figure out what you want.

Consider the art of photography. To capture in photographs those sensitive, heart-touching moments that rival poetry with their power, you must use the camera daily, photographing the mundane, the casual, the ordinary. Why? Because if you wait for that rare, precious moment before you reach for the camera, it will feel like a ton of strange machinery in your hands. The rare moment will be long gone as you stumble through the technical process. You will not be comfortable or adept at your craft. It is the same with the intuitive knowing and naming of desire: if you wait until the moment of need to connect with your heart, you will feel awkward and desperate in its company. As strange as it may sound, you must *practice* wanting, and specifically naming those wants.

Exercise: *Inventory of Concerns*

Make a list of everything that is on your mind. Write down whatever it is that takes up time in your thought process, from "Put air in front left tire" to "Get a job." Some items may be small and incidental, others may be stressful and anxiety-producing; regardless of their relative importance, put them on the list. You may think the list will never end; keep adding items until you feel you have emptied the current Inventory of Concerns held in your mind.

Exercise: *List of Desires*

Make a list of everything that you want. Include both material items such as a new car, computer, vacation on a tropical island, and accomplishments such as cleaning your kitchen, changing jobs, or learning to speak French. Do not limit yourself by what you believe is possible. For the purposes of this exercise, assume that everything is possible.

Compare your "Inventory of Concerns" with your "List of Desires." How many of your desires are represented in some way in your concerns? Observe the amount of energy and time spent on obligations and responsibilities to others, and how much is spent on your personal desires.

The purpose of this exercise is to assess whether or not you are in touch with your own desires, and further, if you are devoting any focused energy toward manifesting them. I am not suggesting that a person become obsessed with personal goals to the point of insensitivity to others or withdrawal from community. I do believe that most of us ignore our own desires to the detriment of our self-development. When we come to partnerships and groups with a need for attention and nurturing which we, as individuals, must give ourselves, our capacity for truly giving and receiving with others is diminished, and we have inappropriate and unrealistic expectations about what the group can give us. A balance between nurturing personal goals and group goals is the ideal.

One obstacle to aiming that plagues the majority of people seems to be money—or the lack of it. Many of us operate on a tight budget, and when our daydreams seem too outrageous, our internal economist is usually saying, "You'll never have enough money to do that!" At some point, in anticipation of that scolding voice, we cease to name any desire that taxes our budget. Money is only one aspect needed to achieve a goal; if you have everything else you need, money may not be as difficult to find as you think. If money were abundant, what would you want?

Exercise: Money Tree

Have a spending spree in your journal! First, give yourself
$500 and the afternoon to spend it, or allocate it, any
way you wish. What would you do? Describe exactly
what you decide.

Next, give yourself $5,000 and a day to allocate it. This
money is tax-free, and you may do anything you wish
with it. Make a list of your purchases, investments, and
gifts.

Now, give yourself $500,000. You have a week to allocate this sum. You may encounter all sorts of skeptical internal voices wanting to stop you: "You'll never have that much money, why bother? You don't deserve to have these things! You're so selfish! These are foolish things to want! If anyone sees this list, they'll know how greedy you are!" Write these "stopper" voices in the margins of your journal and continue with your financial tasks. Do whatever research is necessary to make your allocations basically accurate. If you want a sailboat, what kind is it and approximately what does it cost? If you want to start a shelter for battered women, list out your start-up costs for the first three months and see how far your money will go. This is an exercise to strengthen your ability to name your desires.

Aiming is the art of naming your destination: where you want to go, who you want to be, what you want to accomplish and have in your life. Aiming is not selfish or self-centered — it is an important extension of self-knowledge. Practice your aim, and when you are ready, you can set your attitude in motion.

Attitude

Attitude asks, "How do I get what I want?" In navigational terms, the attitude of an airplane is its precise and ever-shifting position as the plane moves through space. In personal terms, your attitude refers to the constantly changing strategy necessary to accomplish your aim. Attitude is about making a plan, putting the dreams identified in aiming on paper and targeting them. How far away is that dream? Is it over a mountain range, or across the ocean? Is it just next door, or disguised as another place entirely? How will you get there from here?

Forming your attitude is an act of personal cartography: making a map that charts the path from your current reality to the summit of your goal. As you follow the map, you will undoubtedly discover new aspects of your journey. What you thought was an ocean is a lake; what looked like a mountain is a haystack; what appeared to be a paved road is a deep ravine. You may find you need different tools than when you started out, or that you need to learn new skills to reach your destination. All of this is part of maintaining a flexible attitude.

Unlike your aim which is constant, attitude is about flexibility and change. It compensates for the lessons you learn along the way, integrating the advantages you gain and assessing your mistakes. Attitude fine-tunes your plan so that it continues to honor the aim despite surprises along the way. Attitude assesses and evaluates the progress you make, recording and documenting in order to make strategy . . . and more strategy . . . and more strategy. When you form your attitude, you make a "to-do list" that breaks your aim into a series of absolutely concrete, attainable, manageable tasks. As you accomplish each one, check your aim against your attitude, and adjust your plan accordingly.

The journal is a perfect vehicle for attitude work. Choose a goal, design a plan, date it, and generate a to-do list. In a week, go back to the plan, notice which tasks still remain, celebrate accomplishments, and evaluate progress. Refine the plan, date it, and generate a new task list. Make a long-range plan that estimates a time-line for accomplishing your goal; tab it in the journal so you can refer to it quickly. Keep track of the things you accomplish along the way, and never get attached to a plan: always be ready to change it. A good slogan to keep in mind is "Create and adjust!"

Exercise: *Mapping Forward*

Choose one of the items on your List of Desires and design a plan for it.

1. Name what resources are needed.
2. Name what needs to be done.
3. Name a target date for reaching your goal.
4. Create a to-do list naming all the steps involved and the time each requires.

Here's an example of a plan. My aim is to visit Bryce Canyon, Utah.

Resources needed: Transportation, money, camping equipment, vacation time, companion.

What needs to be done: Research on the canyon (campsites, facilities, seasonal weather conditions, routes, best hiking tours, etc.), get minor repair work done on car, new tires, assess camping equipment, arrange desired vacation time in schedule, start Bryce Canyon savings account, ask Joanne to go with me.

Target date: September 15–30, five months away.

The to-do list will break down the items in the second step into the smallest chores, such as "Go to the library to research canyon," "Contact AAA for an itinerary," "Arrange to borrow sleeping bag from Pam," "Get estimates on car repair." Since I've named my target date, I can put these tasks on a time-line that clearly shows when I need to get each item done, and how it affects the rest of the plan. For example, I've estimated that I'll need $700 for the trip itself, and $400 to do the necessary car repairs. When my mechanic says the work will only cost $175 and offers a deal on tires, four for $125, suddenly I'm $100 closer to my goal. Keeping track of my progress in my journal shows me exactly where I am, and what needs to be done next.

The paradox of attitude work is that the acute awareness of specific, concrete tasks actually encourages spontaneity and flexibility. By maintaining a consciousness of how the current step fits into the overall plan, you cultivate the ability to recognize and take creative advantage of opportunities that arise (frequently in the form of conflict). You are able to troubleshoot obstacles before they become crises. The journal mirrors your progress and keeps you on track.

A word about obstacles: rather than becoming discouraged when you map out your plan and find a few seemingly immovable boulders in your path, consider that obstacles tell you what to do next. They are indicators of stored, blocked energy. When you concentrate creative power on an obstacle, you release a treasure trove of resources that can now align with your aim.

Aiming without attitude is frustrating. Setting goals without a clue of how to attain them sets you up to be tortured by your magnificent dreams, and leaves you feeling like a cowardly failure. Attitude without aim can be obsessive, ungrounded energy, always busy going nowhere—the eternal listmaker never accomplishing anything, the list never ends and the ends are never met. With both tools, you have what you need to design your own future.

INNER VIEW

Imagine five years have passed. The year is _____.
Write an entry for a typical day in your life.

INNER VIEW

If you knew that in one year you would die suddenly, would you change anything about the way you are living now? How and why?

AFTERWORD:
Journalkeeping as a Revolutionary Act

*I*N THE FIRST SCENE of George Orwell's novel *1984,* Winston, the main character, returns to his small apartment with a package. Carefully, Winston positions himself in the one blind spot of the constant video surveillance of Big Brother, and opens the package—a journal of blank pages. He discovered the journal in an antique shop, and purchased it as if it were contraband, for such items were scarce and considered to indicate disloyalty to the government. The act of relating to the self symbolized by journalkeeping was strictly prohibited, and Winston's anxiety and excitement as he expresses his personal thoughts testifies to the seriousness of his offense. So unaccustomed is he to privacy, freedom, and intimacy, he hardly knows what to say. His hand shakes in fear as he risks recording the voice of his essential self. In Orwell's fictional society, the primary means of oppression was the absolute control of information, extending especially to personal expression.

Currently, we are a few years beyond Orwell's "1984," and the society we face is not nearly so grim. But in some ways, our estrangement from self is just as severe, if not governmentally imposed. While Big Brother does not watch us from video screens in every room, television programming with VCR back-up fills our leisure time with mindless images, robbing us of authentic connection—with ourselves, other people, or nature. Computerization depersonalizes more interactions, from banking and bill-paying to shopping and writing. Almost every aspect of work is affected by the abuse of high technology, in most cases removing humans further from meaningful labor and from one another. We suffer from "information glut," as more sophisticated media urges us from every side to consume products designed to fulfill needs we never dreamed we'd have. Twenty-two minutes of news punctuated by advertisements tell us what happened of importance today.

Although such a society offers many conveniences and advantages, there is a danger when the streamlined efficiency of technology is deemed more important than the sometimes awkward unpredictability of interaction with the living. Without a terminal and keyboard between us, will we become uncomfortable in each other's company? Suddenly Orwell's sterile, totalitarian vision becomes a bit too real. If we cannot connect with one another in an authentic, satisfying way, we cannot join together to fight oppression and injustice, or to create a society that affirms life.

Orwell's choice of journalkeeping as the first example of Winston's revolt against Big Brother was no mistake. Self-reflection stimulates awareness, analysis, process, and self-intimacy—all characteristics of a creative perspective that challenges authority and perceives the broadest range of available options in any given situation. While we do not currently face the criminalization of self-empowering activities such as journalkeeping, in some ways such drastic action is unnecessary. Our own internalized oppression, which mirrors the dominant culture's desires, keeps us from pursuing them.

In a strictly individual sense, the practice of journalkeeping for self-intimacy cultivates many positive aspects. Journalkeeping helps us:

○ *Practice and strengthen the skills of self-observation and self-awareness.*
○ *Participate in our own growth and change.*
○ *Integrate our experiences as we have them.*
○ *Hear the deepest internal voice in each moment.*
○ *Identify and clarify moments of choice.*

○ *Bring personal sensitivity to the present moment.*
○ *Create an environment of self-love.*

Obviously, these aspects are beneficial to us as individuals, but this level of self-intimacy is important also in the broader picture of the global community. From many sectors of society, people are calling for a paradigm shift in values if we as a species and as a planet are to survive. Feminists, ecologists, environmentalists, anti-nuclear groups, and others agree on the need for a complete realignment of our priorities away from militarism, dominance, and exploitation. Instead, values that affirm life, such as cooperation, a celebration of diversity, and interconnection with all of nature, offer a path away from destruction.

The reality of such a dramatic shift in global values occurs constantly, but on an individual level. The transition requires that we conscientiously observe ourselves and constantly shed old habits while we cultivate new ones amidst a society that seems hell-bent on following destructive norms. It is in our internal affairs that we will take the first steps toward saving ourselves and the planet. A loving, honest relationship with self cultivated through journalkeeping and other life-affirming activities gives us the power to make our own value judgements, based on a knowledge and awareness of our own being.

So, as odd as it may seem, the work we have done in this book is revolutionary. Use this as a start, find a journal you love, and keep the revolution going.

RESOURCES

CHAPTER 1

Baldwin, Christina. *One to One: Self-Understanding Through Journal Writing*. New York: M. Evans & Co., 1977.

Malone, Thomas, and Malone, Patrick. *The Art of Intimacy*. New York: Prentice Hall, 1987.

CHAPTER 2

Bass, Ellen, and Davis, Laura. *The Courage to Heal: A Guide for Women Survivors of Child Sexual Abuse*. New York: Harper & Row, 1988.

Field, Joanna. *A Life of One's Own*. Los Angeles: J. P. Tarcher, Inc., 1981.

Rainer, Tristine. *The New Diary*. Los Angeles: J. P. Tarcher, Inc., 1978.

Rico, Gabriele Lusser. *Writing the Natural Way*. Los Angeles: J. P. Tarcher, Inc., 1983.

Two Women Boxing. Bookbinders. 3002 Commerce Street, Dallas, TX 75226, (214) 939-1626. *Beautiful journals in paper, leather, soft or hard cover, variety in design. Custom work as well as retail line.*

CHAPTER 3

Macy, Joanna Rogers. *Despair and Personal Power in the Nuclear Age*. Philadelphia: New Society Publishers, 1983.

CHAPTER 4

Butler, Pamela E. *Talking to Yourself: Learning the Language of Self-Support*. San Francisco: Harper & Row, 1981.

Gendlin, Eugene T. *Focusing.* New York: Bantam, 1981.

Goleman, Daniel. *Vital Lies, Simple Truths: The Psychology of Self-Deceit.* New York: Simon & Schuster, 1985.

Woititz, Janet G. *Adult Children of Alcoholics.* Hollywood, Florida: Health Communications, 1983.

CHAPTER 5

Adair, Margo. *Working Inside Out: Applied Meditation for Intuitive Problem-Solving.* San Francisco: Wingbow Press, 1984.

Anthony, Carol. *I Ching.* Stow, MA: Anthony Publishing Co., 1980.

Blum, Ralph. *Book of Runes.* New York: St. Martin's Press, 1982.

Faraday, Ann. *The Dream Game.* New York: Harper & Row, 1974.

Garfield, Patricia. *Creative Dreaming.* New York: Ballantine, 1974.

Greer, Mary K. *Tarot for Yourself.* North Hollywood, CA: Newcastle, 1984.

La Berge, Stephen. *Lucid Dreaming.* New York: Ballantine, 1985.

Mariechild, Diane. *Mother Wit: A Feminist Guide to Psychic Development.* Trumansburg, NY: Crossing Press, 1981.

Noble, Vickie. *Motherpeace: A Way to the Goddess through Myth, Art, and Tarot.* San Francisco: Harper & Row, 1983.

Williams, Strephon Kaplan. *Jungian-Senoi Dreamwork Manual.* Berkeley, CA: Journey Press, 1982.

CHAPTER 6

Koberg, Don, and Bagnall, Jim. *Universal Traveler: A Soft-Systems Guide to Creativity, Problem-Solving and the Process of Reaching Goals.* Los Altos: William Kaufman, Inc., 1976.

Reynolds, David K. *Playing Ball on Running Water.* New York: William Morrow & Co., 1984.

Sanford, Linda Tschirhardt, and Donovan, Mary Ellen. *Women and Self-Esteem: Understanding and Improving the Way We Think and Feel about Ourselves.* New York: Viking Penguin, 1984.

CHAPTER 7

See Chapter 6. Koberg, Don, and Bagnall, Jim.

Sher, Barbara, and Gottilieb, Annie. *Wishcraft: How to Get What You Really Want.* New York: Ballantine, 1979.

Sinetar, Marsha. *Do What You Love, the Money Will Follow.* New York: Paulist Press, 1987.

ACKNOWLEDGMENTS

*T*HE IDEAS IN THIS BOOK evolved in workshops taught over eight years. Without the questions, stories, and trust of the people who participated in both my journalkeeping workshops and Feminars, there would have been no book. My deep appreciation to all of you.

In addition, many friends assisted me in countless ways. Edie Cohen was a tireless, loving editor who miraculously coaxed an unruly batch of transcripts into a coherent manuscript, and stayed with me to the end. Joanne DeMark put this book on my to-do list in a way I could understand, and lent emotional, financial, and spiritual support. Linda Finnell relentlessly insisted this book was important. Drue Waible loaned her computer to me for three weeks and let me keep it for three months. The Websters—Feral Willcox, Amanda Gable, Celeste Tibbets, Leslita Williams, and Debra Hiers—gave me weekly encouragement and excellent critiques in our writers' group. KC Wildmoon enriched the first edition of the book with her typesetting and design skills. Linda Bryant, Red Crowley, Bill Eisenhauer, June Bryant, Dirgha Darshi, Nina Klebanoff, the women of Charis Books and More, Jayne Pleasants, Judith Harriss, and Richard Downing all gave me crucial help at critical times. Cathy McHenry, Carol Harrison, Pam Leonard, Edith Pula, Nancy Kavanaugh, Paula Burgess, Diane Fowlkes, Delores Gohring, Carolyn Rapp, Drue Waible,

Lynn Magner, Linda Bryant, Deborah Baldridge, Apollonia Fortino, Randy Stepp, and Winifred Adams formed a special circle of support for my efforts.

Special thanks for an early start to Lillian T. Rhodes.